MW00636049

Who Moved the Line?

America's Character Crisis

Who Moved the Line?

America's Character Crisis

by

Amie Beth Dickinson

with Denise George

Buck Publishing Company
Birmingham, Alabama

Who Moved the Line?
by Amie Beth Dickinson and Denise George

Buck Publishing Company
2409 Vestavia Drive
Birmingham, Alabama 35216

Printed in the United States

Library of Congress Catalog Card Number: 96-086502
ISBN 0-934530-10-6

Cover Photo Credit - David Bartley Photography

Contents

Acknowledgements

I have been blessed by so many people to whom I want to express my gratitude:

First, my Mom and Dad. You have given me a beautiful life. I can't thank you enough for your tremendous support and love. I wish all kids could be so fortunate.

My brother and sister. You are dear to me. You were such good sports the last few years. Chip, at least you don't have to go to any more pageants. Arden, you are my eternal Christmas present. I love you both.

Nana and Grandpa. You're two of the finest grandparents a girl could have. You are the ultimate example of wisdom and compassion for a family. And to the entire Wills-Dickinson clan (there are a bunch of us), I greatly appreciate your support—letters, phone calls, and pageant watching! I have the best family. If others could meet you all, they'd want to be a part of the family, too.

Maureen Duran. If I had a big sister, you'd be it! You are both friend and mentor. You lent me your words, your time, and your love. What an inspiration and blessing you have been.

Eleanor Trafton. I'm very grateful for the hours and hours you invested in practicing and talking, talking and practicing—and encouraging. You are a dear friend, mentor, and teacher. I love you.

Stephen Ball and Allen Bennett. I never thought I would meet two awesome guys like you. The time we spent rehearsing, interviewing, and eating are priceless memories.

Dr. Frank Barker, Dr. Byrle Kynerd, and the Briarwood

Presbyterian church and school family. You provided me with a solid foundation. Each new day, I am more and more appreciative of you as role models and the life lessons I learned while in your care.

My pageant family—the Miss Alabama board, pageant staff, new pageant friends, judges, directors, sponsors. From the bottom of my heart, I thank you for giving me a chance to be "my best self." You all provided an atmosphere that challenged me in every way. Your caring and encouragement is a lifelong legacy.

Lest I not forget, my precious traveling companions. You gave your time and lives. You offered friendship and guidance. No one else would have listened to my speeches as much as you did.

Mark and Norma Roessler and the Catalina Foothills church. You have a special place in my heart. Mark, you helped me see all sides of an issue and speak more quickly on my feet.

Three friends have been instrumental in bringing me to this point. Kimberlee Dawkins Thompson, you provided the inspiration for my platform. So actually all of this is your fault. (Just kidding!) Aimee Barrett Hay, if it weren't for your courage, I would not be speaking. You provided that first opportunity at Auburn University. Kimberly Till Lisenby, your organizational skills are commendable. You kept me together and designed that excellent community service book. I love you all.

This book would be nowhere, actually still just an idea, if it weren't for Denise George. You spent time in research and helped me put my thoughts into words. And Bill and Janie Buck and Mary Ann Appling. You helped edit the book and guide it through the publishing process. I cannot begin to adequately express my gratitude, so I will say a heartfelt thanks.

Bo Stanford and American Printing. What a friend! You gave us confidence that the book would be done on time. And it was!

Taylor and Samford University classmates and professors. Thanks for being patient as my speaking often called me elsewhere.

My biological parents. Thank you for making a difficult decision. It would have been so easy for you to choose otherwise.

My Lord and Savior, Jesus Christ, I am grateful for your sacrifice and your love. I don't know how people make it without you.

Dedication

To my Mom and Dad,
Doug and Barbara Dickinson,

and to the women
who gave us our family.

CHAPTER 1
Hard Decisions

On a warm August morning, in a small Pennsylvania hospital, a frightened seventeen-year-old, unmarried and alone, gave birth to a baby girl.

She had been through a nine-month nightmare after the pregnancy test proved positive. Terrified, she faced difficult decisions:

Should she tell her boyfriend about his child?

If he wanted to marry, were they ready?

How should she tell her parents?

Could someone her age raise a baby alone? Was there any hope for a secure future without a job or education?

These were hard questions.

She had another alternative. For the first time in the United States, abortions were legal. This seemed to be a simple way out to a frightened, lonely girl. After all, the Supreme Court in *Roe v. Wade* had given legal permission for a woman to rid herself of an unplanned or inconvenient pregnancy.

She couldn't ignore her expanding waistline or the changes in her small body as, day by day, the child grew. This girl, still in high school and slowly developing into womanhood, had to make a tough decision—quickly.

In fact, this would be the hardest choice of her life. It would not only affect her and the child as long as they lived, but also the father and both their parents. This brave teenager decided not to kill her child but carry it full-term and give birth in a county hospital. She hoped a loving couple would adopt her newborn as their own.

It was a wise and correct decision. But it was very hard. In tears, this young mother gave up the daughter she never saw or held. In spite of deep emotional pain, she turned over the newborn to others.

Her selfless action and her personal sacrifice proved her deep love for her first-born child.

I am that child.

CHAPTER 2

The Line

Lindsay smiled into the mirror and ran a brush through her strawberry-blonde hair. "Hi Jason!" she said, flipping the curls back over her shoulder. "Well, hello, Jason," lowering her voice alluringly. "Jason!" Lindsay giggled as she practiced to her reflection. Which smile should she use when greeting him at the door for their long-awaited first date?

She had admired him from a distance since the beginning of her sophomore year and thought he would never ask her out. He was new in town then and the hottest guy in high school. It was easy to see why. He was the starting running back on the football team and drove a bright red 4x4. She examined her hair, thinking about how it would look blowing in the wind as they drove through town together.

Lindsay and Abbey, her best friend, had spent a day at the mall searching for the perfect outfit. (After casually quizzing his friends, she discovered he had a penchant for blue.) They were both delighted to find a tight-fitting blue sweater they thought would knock his socks off. She now smoothed it with her hands, turning her body left and right to see how she looked. Then she ran her palms over her stomach, sucking in, trying in vain to push away the butterflies of excitement.

So, there she was, looking great, waiting eagerly for the doorbell to ring. It's not often she was ready for a date half an hour early. Her mind started to wander. "I wonder if he'll like me? Maybe we'll start dating and fall in love. Maybe..."

Lindsay wanted to make a lasting impression. An "I'll call you tomorrow" when Jason, hopefully, would kiss her at the door. But she overlooked a major decision about the evening—or any future dates. She planned all the outer details but failed to consider the inner issue in many teenage male-female relationships.

Will she or won't she? What part will sex play on this date or in their potential relationship? If the issue doesn't come up this night, will it later? What will she say or do?

Lindsay has never considered the consequences of teenage sexual activity nor ever drawn the "line in the sand" and determined not to cross it—no matter what! She has not consciously made the decision, "I will not have sex. I will wait until marriage." No moral nor practical stand has ever crossed her mind. There has been no advance planning about what to do when a decision must be made.

Many of her friends are already sexually active. They've told her about their experiences. Some brag in glowing terms. Others are evasive. "Sure, I've done it." But they won't give specifics. Have they really had sex or are they just talking? The only reason she's still a virgin is lack of opportunity. The right moment, the right guy hasn't come along. But she hasn't considered that any moment prior to "I do" is the wrong moment. Yet, she thinks she's prepared for her big night out.

In reality, Lindsey knows very little about the things that really matter about Jason—his character, behavior, and values. She's ready for the date but not ready for the potential aftermath of her behavior, tonight or some time in the future.

People like Lindsay roam the halls of every middle school and high school in America. Their ages, circumstances, and personalities vary. But they're there. And they don't realize they're facing one of the biggest decisions of their lives when confronted with the opportunity to have sex for the first time.

Or the second time, the third time, or each time thereafter. It's a major decision. What happens afterwards can affect their entire lives.

But Lindsay doesn't think about consequences, only friends and fun, acceptance and approval, good times and good looks. She also broods about insecurity and inferiority, awkwardness and awful fears about standing out or being "different." Whether an action is right or wrong doesn't occupy space on her mental horizon. That line in the sand is irrelevant. She doesn't see it because none of her friends have drawn it. If she were aware of it, it would divide right from wrong, good character from bad character, what's moral from what's immoral. It's missing for today's youth. ***Who moved the line?***

Where did it go?

It used to be as obvious and visible as a line painted down the highway separating traffic. Just about everyone knew where the line was placed regarding behavior. Everyone agreed some things were just plain right and others plainly wrong. The line was not gray either, or fuzzy or mobile. What was right was right and wrong was wrong. Sex outside of marriage fell on the wrong side of the line. So did drugs, alcohol, and smoking.

Of course, some have always tried to sneak across the line. And there were a few who openly flaunted it. They didn't think it applied to them. But most people thought those who crossed the line had a character problem. If you had good character, you protected it. Shame and blame followed people who crossed the moral line.

Then something odd happened. It wasn't obvious at first, but the line moved—just a tiny fraction of an inch—in people's minds. No one realized it at the time. The newspapers didn't announce in big headlines, "The line moved today." It didn't make the evening newscast on television.

Then, on another day, the line crept over just another iota. No one seemed to notice this time. There was no public outcry, no one called a big meeting to make plans to move it back. Over a period of years, the line edged a little here, a little there, until today many people don't know it exists. "What line?" they ask. "Why do we need a line anyhow? I'm doing just fine."

Just fine? Is that how we explain the AIDS epidemic? The teenage pregnancy problem that has blown through the roof? Drug and alcohol abuse, and the crime connected with both?

A few months ago, I noticed T-shirts in an advertising mailer from a major retailer, a place where you and I often shop. The words I *make my own rules* were plastered across the front of the shirts. Hmmm. Where does that get you? And what about the rest of us who are affected by your behavior?

A world in which people make their own rules based on what feels good is a world without lines. Too many teenagers have been led to believe they can make their own rules.

Not long after I saw the T-shirt ad, a leading telecommunications company ran an ad campaign with the slogan, "Imagine a World Without Limits." Perhaps the company had good intentions and was referring to communication barriers coming down. But this slogan speaks volumes about a mindset in our society. Many people seek a world without limits regarding their behavior. They don't want to be hemmed in by a line that defines good character. It seems too restricting and reminds them of loss of personal freedom.

We all have to make basic choices about our behavior if we want to have a standard of conduct based on good character principles. The line that distinguishes good character from bad comes with restrictions and limits. You and I are not free to do whatever we want, whenever we choose, with whoever happens to be convenient or agreeable.

But living within the line that defines good character traits offers another kind of freedom—freedom from heartache and despair.

Without thinking, we adhere to lines in our daily routines. We start young. Children in elementary school learn to form a line to walk to the cafeteria. Without the line, there would be chaos in the halls.

There are lines in other areas. When I go to the mall, I have no trouble identifying the difference between a parking space and the road. I park my car between two white lines that mark a legitimate parking space. When I leave, I know where to exit the mall because a line divides the right side of the road from the left.

Have you ever heard people complain their freedom is inhibited because parking lots have spaces marked off with lines? No, we're grateful they're present. Without them, we'd see a free-for-all at every shopping center. Those lines provide comfort and order. I don't want anyone to move them.

All sporting venues—football fields, basketball courts, baseball diamonds—are framed by lines. They are placed at regulation distances based on official rules of the sport. I've never heard a football player complain that the lines marking off the field are too restrictive or inhibit his freedom. Instead, they are commonly agreed upon and respected. No quarterback wishes the goal line would stretch out into the parking lot so his team will have more running room. Can you imagine the outrage at a major bowl game if someone decided to move it a few inches?

Or what about a tennis match? Perhaps at Wimbledon, a player has trouble keeping the ball inside the court. "If I could just move the lines of this court a few feet outward, I wouldn't be having this problem. Maybe no one would notice." Sorry! The line stays.

We accept lines at sporting events, so why not in other arenas of life?

Definitely not normal

Our society is experiencing a cultural free-for-all, much like a parking lot without lines. Never before in the history of the United States has a generation of teenagers had to deal with such an unhealthy sexual culture imposed by people who are supposed to be mature. *Adults* write the scripts for television shows and movies. *Adults* commit infidelity in one-third to one-half of all marriages. *Adults* sexually abuse hundreds of children per day. And *adults* spend time in court because of sexual harassment charges.

Every day we see the results of our culture's preoccupation with sex. It reveals itself in teenage pregnancies, the astronomical number of abortions, rampant drug usage, the AIDS crisis, and epidemics of sexually transmitted diseases.

Why do we accept this as normal? It's definitely abnormal! It's a character crisis! People with good character do not engage in behavior that produces these outcomes. They refuse to cross the line. They have values.

But the word *values* has disappeared from the vocabulary of many people. The term *character* applies to some goofus on TV. What went wrong? What caused this? Who moved the line? Where did it go?

Character is really what you are when no one else is looking. Scary, huh? But it doesn't have to be.

I was fortunate to grow up in a family that taught me right from wrong. As a result, I did not unwittingly find myself in situations which led me in the wrong direction. I'm grateful for the example my parents, teachers, and role models set for me. But character is more than something you simply inherit; it requires your own personal resolve.

Everyone needs to deal with this. I know I've had to. I realized I had to come to a personal decision about my own character.

There comes a point in every teenager's life when you have to determine what kind of person you will be. I had to make some basic decisions that would define my personal character and the standards I would live by. One issue involved sex.

My parents have always been open with me on this subject. My parents' teaching was reinforced when someone came to my high school to talk about the importance of teenagers waiting until marriage to have their first sexual experiences. This made a lot of sense. I decided then to remain a virgin until my wedding night.

Willing to wait

I'm in my twenties now, out of college, and I have not had sex yet. I will one day, when I'm married. I want to commit to one special man who'll love me enough to refrain from sex in our relationship until we say "I do." At that point, we will! I truly believe we'll be glad we waited before knowing each other in this most intimate way. We'll have a relationship based on love and respect, not just physical attraction.

A relationship built solely on sex will not last. I'll never forsake my virginity until a person loves me enough to spend the rest of his life with me.

I've heard people say, "You're twenty-four, and you've never had sex? Get real!" People have laughed at me and told me they've never met anyone my age who wasn't sexually active. I tell them, "Well, you have now."

Please understand I'm not saying this is easy. I've dated a lot. I know the temptations. I've been very lonely. I've been engaged. I've dated guys who have proposed. But I know where the line is, and I have *rationally* considered the consequences of sex outside of marriage. Good decisions can't be made when it's just the two of you and hormones are raging.

It's interesting how often this subject has come up in casual conversation when I've been on a date. I don't know why, but it just has. I've never gone on a first date and said at the beginning, "In case you're wondering, hey, I'm not going to sleep with you." But the subject has come up at some point, and we have talked about where we stood.

Unfortunately, it's rare for a guy to bring up the subject. There are exceptions. One special guy I dated told me at the beginning where he drew the line morally. I deeply respected him for this. Our relationship flourished because of the type of person he was and the fact that he was willing to set high standards.

I don't want to imply that all the responsibility falls on the guys. It should be mutual. If a young woman wants to be treated like a queen, she needs to act like a queen. I love the old saying, "Don't advertise goods that aren't for sale."

Too often, girls are not willing to wait for that quality kind of guy. They settle for so much less. And they get in over their heads in attempts to meet deep emotional needs.

This reminds me of Courtney. She had high standards about dating. But she wanted to be in love, to date one guy exclusively, to have a soulmate and best friend. Then she met Jared. Her parents didn't like him. And he didn't fit in with her regular friends. But Courtney and Jared hit it off and enjoyed long talks. He listened and she felt comfortable sharing her heart. He, too, bared his soul. Sounds basically fine, right? A friend talking to a friend.

It didn't stop there. They became emotionally dependent and physically intimate. She immediately knew it was wrong. But she didn't want to hurt him by saying no after she had already said yes. She didn't want to add to the rejection he had already faced in other areas of life. So, she settled for a relationship that made her miserable.

He had a chip on his shoulder and was emotionally damaged from way back. She couldn't fix him. Long conversations and frequent sex couldn't undo the damage from his home life. She felt isolated from her other friends and wanted out. He wasn't the type of person with whom she wanted to spend the rest of her life.

But Courtney didn't know how to break it off. Teenage sex often creates this problem.

I wish I could talk to every girl like Courtney and tell her there is a way out. I would like to help them clarify their stand about sexual issues.

That's one reason I'm writing this book. I remember the impact of hearing the truth about teenage sex. As a result, I want to communicate some important facts everyone needs to know before, or after, becoming sexually involved.

This can be a life-and-death matter. Even if you do not die

from AIDS or another sexually transmitted disease, there are other problems that come out of premature sex. You may be forsaking the potential for a happy, fulfilled life if you become sexually active as an unmarried teenager.

We've all been there

Remember Lindsay? Did you identify with her? We've all been there, getting ready for a big date. It doesn't matter how old you are. Each of us has been at the front end of a relationship, eager to be liked, wanting to be cool. But for many years, people embarking on new relationships knew where the line should be regarding personal behavior.

In the sixties, the line started moving. It became easier for people like Lindsay to ignore the outcomes stemming from their actions. Or so they thought. As the line moved, it was followed by millions of unplanned pregnancies, abortions, sexually transmitted diseases, AIDS, emotional devastation, as well as alcohol and drug abuse. The character crisis which has invaded our culture has highlighted these issues. Your personal character, and mine, do make a difference.

Every person in America needs to consider these implications. No one is immune from the consequences of his or her own behavior—not teenagers, single adults, married couples, or divorced adults.

If you're a teenager reading this book, you have your future to consider. You may be younger or older than Lindsay. You may still be a virgin, or you might have already taken the sexual plunge. In either case, you need to take a close look at your character and behavior. Are you doing things you suspect or know are wrong? Would you be ashamed for the important people in your life to know what happens when you are alone with a member of the opposite sex? What can you expect from your behavior? You can make a commitment to change. Others have done it. You can, too. But you must have the courage to act. Talk or wishes are just not enough.

Perhaps you are the parent of a teen. In the following pages, you will find some important facts to share with your daughter or son about what happens when young people engage in premature sexual activity. There is still time for you to have a positive impact in your family. It's very important for your children to determine where to draw the line from the safe base of home.

Let's say you're a teacher, pastor, or youth leader. You're in a unique position to highlight character-developing principles for the kids who view you as a role model. You have an arena of influence. In the following pages, you can become better informed about the issues affecting today's kids. You can also consider how you can incorporate character education in your classroom or program.

The issues in this book are serious. There is a character crisis in America. Consider the information in these pages and then take positive action in your own life. You can do something about your behavior, no matter who you are. Begin by asking, who really moved the line?

CHAPTER 3

When Children Have Children

The line has moved. Shame and stigma are no longer attached to unplanned pregnancies. But this event can devastate a teenager's life, cause untold heartaches, and interrupt future plans.

I have met girls only eleven and twelve years old who are expecting babies. Little girls, who should be playing with dolls, are being plunged into parenthood. They haven't begun to wear make-up, and their small bodies have not developed enough to turn them into young women. They are children who still cover their beds with stuffed animals and sit cross-legged on the floor telling ghost stories at slumber parties.

Sex should be farthest from their minds. But children are having children. It's heartbreaking. Unplanned pregnancies are nothing new, but the rate is increasing. Most girls who choose to give birth, instead of having abortions, keep and rear their offspring. Only a small percentage put their babies up for adoption.

Kate was fourteen when she met Dave. He was popular,

especially with the beer drinkers and marijuana smokers. She liked him, and they began dating exclusively. After several dates, they decided to become sexually intimate. Dave used condoms, but Kate still became pregnant. Though unmarried, Kate elected to keep and raise her daughter, Michelle.

"I didn't drop out of school," Kate says, "but I felt awkward. I lost some good friends."

Nine years later, she and her daughter still live with Kate's parents. Keeping an exhausting schedule, Kate works during the day and attends college at night. She missed much of the fun of her teenage years. She was saddled with heavy adult responsibilities.

I'll never forget the young girl who stopped my dad and me in a parking lot after one of my talks about teenage sexuality and pregnancy. She was a tiny thirteen-year-old.

"Amie Beth, can we talk?" she asked.

"Sure," I answered.

She said, "I really wish I had heard you two years ago."

I asked, "Why?"

"Because this is my baby." She held a beautiful little girl in her arms. "My name is Rachel," she told me, "and this is my daughter, Raven."

My heart broke as I looked at that thirteen-year-old child holding her own baby.

"I really wish I had heard you," she said again as we waved good-bye.

When she left, my dad and I closed our car doors and cried.

Reasons why

Never before have teenagers been forced to deal with overwhelming problems created by an unhealthy sexual culture perpetuated by adults. It sends confusing messages concerning teen sexual behavior. Experts state babies born to teenage mothers are more likely to be abused. They are often the ones who are held back in school, have behavioral and emotional disorders, and become drug-addicted and teenage parents themselves.[1]

Early sexual activity results from a strong need to love and be loved. Unfortunately, this lack of love at home leads to sexual indulgence and irresponsibility. Most teens aren't looking for sexual relationships. They're looking for love. Those who claim to truly love their partners but engage in premature sex are fooling themselves. A person who truly loves doesn't jeopardize the other person's physical, mental, or emotional health.

There are some who indulge in sex because they wrongly believe that sex will make the relationship stronger. This never happens.

Others believe they can "prove" their love to a partner if sex is involved. Early sex, in reality, tends to break up relationships. All it really proves is that the people involved are loveless, guilt-filled, and lack self-control. This leads to depression and even suicide.

Teens may become sexually active because they think "everybody's doing it." They want to fit in with the crowd. But *everybody* is not doing it. Sexual activity sets them *apart* from the crowd, especially if they become pregnant or acquire a sexually transmitted disease.

One girl describes her experience: "It's not a pretty picture, sex outside of marriage. It's scary, and it's lonely.... Sex was my choice one hot summer night. It made me face many decisions I thought I would never have to make. Those decisions radically changed my life."

A teenage girl may engage in sex in an effort to keep her boyfriend. When I speak, I often read a letter that tells a common story:

> About two and one half years ago, Mr. Right came along. Unlike the fairy tale, my dream boy lover turned out to be a nightmare. I am twenty now, and the fact that someone knows me inside and out still hurts after two years. I had to learn the hard way that sex before marriage is not smart. If

you have to have sex with someone just to keep him, he is not worth keeping.

I often quote these poems:

A Woman's Poem
I met him; I liked him.
I liked him; I loved him.
I loved him; I let him.
I let him; I lost him.

A Man's Poem
I saw her; I liked her.
I loved her; I wanted her.
I asked her; She said no!
I married her.
After 60 years, I still have her.[2]

Difference between sex and love

Most teenagers I'm acquainted with are confused about the difference between sex and love. Sex education programs mainly focus on the physical. Teens are not aware of the powerful emotional aspects.

I wish I had the attention and ear of every teenager. I would tell them that when you have sex, you bond with your partner in a way unlike any other bonding you can have. Sex compels an intimate giving of yourself to the other person. Sex unites the two souls as well as their bodies. In essence, each becomes a part of the other.

Genital bonding should occur only when you are married and love the person deeply. But it can also occur whether or not you like each other. Or, I'm sorry to say, if you hate one another, as in rape. Unlike physical bonding, which lasts only for the moment of the actual act, emotional bonding remains.

Couples also bond intellectually, morally, and socially.

When one party tries to end this union, the other experiences pain. Once a couple has shared these intimate physical parts of themselves, they can never get them back. A portion of one person will remain attached to the other.

A closer look

Love is more than a feeling. Feelings come and go. Some teens believe if they are "in love," then it's okay to have sex. Society sends false messages to youth about the meaning of this emotion. Young men and women define it differently.

Ray E. Short, professor of sociology at the University of Wisconsin says:

> There is a biological reason why boys and girls define love differently. Once puberty occurs boys may build up sexual fluids every two to three days. Usually the boys are able to eliminate the pressure of sexual fluids naturally, through nocturnal emissions. Boys reach the peak of their sexual interest between 17 and 19 years of age. At this time their sexual drive is urgent.
>
> Young women may reach their sexual peak at 28 years of age and older. Young women usually have a stronger desire for signs of affection—such as holding hands, hugging, etc. They want to hear words of love, etc. By this age, most young women already have a strong desire for romantic love. For the young woman, love is not the same as sex. Girls usually take sexual relationships more seriously than boys.
>
> There tends to be some confusion, therefore, about the word "love." In their teens young men and young women often define love differently. The old saying may be true. Boys use love to get sex and girls use sex to get love. However, if the girl is sexually aroused, she will have a strong

> desire for sex. It's easier to arouse a boy, because his genitals are external. A girl may take longer to arouse because her genitals are internal. Unfortunately, when a young couple defines love differently they may unintentionally use each other because they think that they are in love.[3]

I wish I could convince teens of the big difference between sex and love. For sex to be its best and most fulfilling, it must take place in the context of marriage. Otherwise, it is not real love, just lust.

Real love is not some feeling as described in romantic songs. Feelings should not be the source of rational decisions.

How do I define real love? The best definition I've found, in a book that means a lot to me, states:

> Love is very patient and kind, never jealous or envious, never boastful or proud. Never haughty or selfish or rude. Love does not demand its own way. It is not irritable or touchy. It does not hold grudges and will hardly even notice when others do it wrong. It is never glad about injustice, but rejoices whenever truth wins out. If you love someone you will be loyal to him no matter what the cost. You will always believe in him, always expect the best of him, and always stand your ground in defending him. All the special gifts and powers from God will someday come to an end, but love goes on forever (1 Cor. 13:4-8 ***The Living Bible***).

A mature person who understands love would not involve someone in a harmful activity, such as sex outside of marriage.

The only responsible sexual activity is based on fidelity, commitment, and maturity—within the context of marriage. This kind of love is wonderful but sometimes hard to find. Couples who discover it usually spend much time together. They share happy as well as sad experiences and learn to solve their problems. They develop mutual interests and each considers the other person's needs as important as his or her own.

Then, when married, sex becomes the expression of their love. It serves as the perfect bonding of the marriage relationship. This is sex that is fulfilling. It is the kind of sexual love relationship in which pregnancy becomes a blessing and not a burden. A new life is excitedly anticipated, not dreaded.

This kind of love, this kind of sex, is a far cry from anything known by a thirteen-year-old holding baby Raven in a parking lot or an unmarried seventeen-year-old crying into her pillow at night, afraid to tell her parents she's pregnant.

It hurts

Young people are the victims of the sexual revolution that started in the late twentieth century, or the "intimacy revolution," as I call it. Sex is an area of life that often brings with it tremendous emotional pain. It is a display case for the poorest character traits: lack of respect, responsibility, and self-control.

What is really happening in the intimacy revolution?

An incredible number of high school students are having to endure sexual harassment during school hours.[4]

For example, in Indiana, a high school teacher says, "The air is thick with sex talk. Kids in the halls will say—boy to girl, girl to boy—'I want to f—- you.'"

At Lakewood High School, in an affluent Los Angeles suburb, boys formed a club called a Spur Posse. Members competed over how many girls they had slept with. The club's leader claimed sixty-three. Two members were arrested after molesting a ten-year-old.

In a small town in upstate New York, a sixth-grade teacher comments: "The boys bring in **Playboy**, the girls wear make-up and jewelry, and the kids write sexual notes to each other." In a fourth-grade class, boys wrote girls notes saying, "I love you. Let's have sex."

Half of the students in a Rhode Island school considered it

acceptable for a man to force sex on a woman if they had been dating six months or more.[5]

The sexual liberation?

Since the sixties, what many call sexual liberation has only produced bondage. Teens have been pressured to try out activities once reserved for marriage. As a result, they have to cope with adult responsibility.

Is this liberation? Hardly.

My own state, Alabama, has one of the highest percentage of births to teens in the nation.[6]

Why all the unplanned pregnancies with their devastating consequences? Here are a few of the reasons:

• The adult sexual culture is out of control. Child sexual abuse is on the rise, and sexual harassment cases are filling up the courts.

• Poverty and broken families lead some teens to seek love and status by having babies.[7]

• Our society perpetuates an "anything-goes" moral climate.

• Babies are born out of wedlock and hardly anyone blinks. Society is unwilling to affirm and support the values and benefits of marriage.

• Our culture supports a rising rate of sexual promiscuity because sex is exploited as a glittering commodity.

• Teens feel extraordinary peer pressure and the need to prove themselves sexually.

• People have an overwhelming desire for close emotional intimacy.

• The media uses sex to advertise everything from perfume to cars, detergent to toothpaste! It promotes sexual activity as a common lifestyle for the young.

What all this boils down to is standards, or really the lack of them, personally and culturally. But teen pregnancy is not the only issue where this is evident. It's everywhere. Do you ever wonder if anyone else cares?

CHAPTER 4

The Tragedy

Some stories are so horrible they are difficult to believe. The following is that kind of story, and it is true. It's about a doctor who performs abortions. I'll call him Dr. Clark, and he admits to killing more than 60,000 to 70,000 unborn babies.

His patient is Mary, a young mother with five small children. When she became pregnant again, she visited Dr. Clark's abortion clinic.

Sue was the doctor's assistant, and it was her job to evaluate the patient to determine if she was a proper candidate for an elective abortion. Due to several medical factors, Sue did not recommend surgery.

Dr. Clark reacted to Sue's decision, "What the h—- is going on? Why are you turning that patient down? You know we need the money. Just put her through."

So Sue prepped Mary for surgery, and Dr. Clark performed the abortion. Then he left the room with Mary still under general anesthesia.

Something went wrong. The pulse oximeter alarm buzzed loudly, and the non-invasive blood pressure alarm sounded.

Sue set the machine to retake Mary's blood pressure. She recalled, "The alarm sounded and zeros came up on the digital readout. I got a regular blood pressure cuff and a stethoscope, and I sent [another worker] after Dr. Clark."

He returned, and Sue reported she could not obtain a blood pressure plus the patient was "having difficulty breathing." Dr. Clark's office was not equipped with proper anesthesia resuscitation equipment so he had to resort to mouth-to-mouth.

Dr. Clark administered various drugs, although he did not chart the doses.

Sue recalls, "Mary appeared to stabilize somewhat. We could again hear the blood pressure although it was still very low. These blood pressure readings were never recorded.... The pulse oximeter kept going off and sounding its alarm.

"Dr. Clark said: 'Turn that d—- thing off. The patients next door can hear it.'"

Sue turned it off.

Mary was breathing on her own but, at this point, began gasping for breath. Dr. Clark instructed Sue to take the patient to the back recovery room.

The only equipment in the recovery room was a portable oxygen tank. Dr. Clark ordered intravenous medication, but Sue told him she had not been trained to administer that particular drug, so Dr. Clark did it himself.

"Mary had started hemorrhaging," Sue recalls. "Dr. Clark instructed me to . . . examine her to see if I could see where the bleeding was coming from."

She took the patient to the exam room, saw that the blood appeared to be coming from the uterus, and packed her with four-by-four sterile gauze pads.

Sue goes on with her story: "At that time, I called the ambulance. I felt Mary was dying and needed to go to the hospital immediately. I went back into the exam room to get Mary ready for the transfer to the hospital. Dr. Clark came into the room very angry.

"He said, 'I'm the G— d—- doctor here. If anybody's going to call the f——— ambulance, it will be me!'

"He informed me that he had canceled the ambulance.

"During Dr. Clark's presence, I took Mary's blood pressure

again and I told Dr. Clark that I could not hear anything. He came around behind me and did the blood pressure.

"He said: 'You just didn't pump it up high enough. She's OK, just keep giving her this medicine.'

"Dr. Clark walked out of the room and [another worker] said to me, 'Sue, he's lying. He did not hear that blood pressure. He's panicked and you'd better do something. This patient is going to lay right here and die.'"

Sue remained with Mary. She remembers, "The bleeding came through the packing .... The blood was draining down the exam table and onto the floor, and up the exam table under Mary's back, soaking the sheets and her gown with blood. I tried to stop the bleeding, but it was just flowing like a faucet."

Sue frantically found Dr. Clark to report the bleeding.

"What the h—- do you want me to do about it?" he replied.

Sue told him: "We've got to get her to the hospital or she's going to die."

"Fine," Dr. Clark said, "call the G— d—- ambulance!"

Then he walked out of the building.

Sue returned to the exam room, replaced the packing, changed Mary's gown and sheets, and cleaned the room . She didn't want the paramedics to see how much blood had been lost.

Before the ambulance came, recalls Sue, Mary's blood pressure "bottomed out. Breathing ... became even more difficult ... . I called Dr. Clark on his car phone. I told him that I couldn't get a blood pressure and he told me to administer the medication again, and I told him that I didn't want to. He said, 'Just administer the medication!'"

The ambulance came and transported Mary to a nearby hospital.

She died two days later.

But that's not the end of the story.

"Sometime later," Sue recalled, "a subpoena came from the [state] Medical Licensing Board for Mary's record. Dr. Clark told me to pull Mary's chart and go into my office. Dr. Clark said, 'We need to review and change these records.'

"We went through each sheet in Mary's chart, step by step, and Dr. Clark decided what he wanted to keep in the chart and what he wanted to change.

"'If you want to keep your job,' he told me, 'you'll do it!'"

Sue changed the records as instructed. She removed pages, and Dr. Clark tore them up. He tried burning them in his ashtray. but the smoke detector went off. That's when he put the pieces in a brown sack, handed the bag to Sue, and ordered her to finish burning them in the basement.

Sue didn't burn the sheets. Instead, she pieced them together and handed them over to an attorney when Mary's family brought legal action against Dr. Clark.

This is a true story.[1] I have changed the names of the individuals involved, but the facts came from a legal affidavit filed in a court of law. It is available for public viewing at the courthouse. Some people may think this story is an exception, but I don't. The killing of babies is despicable, but mothers, these poor teenage mothers, are often maimed for life, and death occurs too often. It is happening all over the United States.

Health Hazard

Abortions are often performed in secret with few and haphazardly kept records. It is not unusual for patients to pay with large sums of untraceable cash.

It's frightening that abortionists are not closely scrutinized by their medical peers. A physical exam may or may not precede the abortion, and women often receive no follow-up. Clinic workers are not sufficiently trained to handle acute emergencies. Many of them have only high school diplomas.

This report by Candace C. Crandall which appeared in the Wall Street Journal is very revealing:

> Women are dying from abortion. And they are dying not because of good doctors making honest mistakes but because of bad doctors taking calculated risks.

Just how much bad medicine is being glossed over in the name of choice? "A lot," according to Warren Hern, a nationally known specialist in abortion and author of "Abortion Practice," the nation's most widely used textbook on the subject. Epidemiologists with the federal Centers for Disease Control and Prevention will say only that they cannot be certain that all abortion-related deaths are being reported. But today, anyone can sit down at a computer—as I did recently—and pull up hundreds of newspaper accounts of death, injury, and fraud at walk-in abortion clinics across the country.

These are not the pristine establishments where Radcliffe girls might go for a weekend abortion. These are the clinics that advertise in Spanish-language newspapers and neighborhood weeklies, pay kickbacks to sleazy phone referral services, and lure women through the doorway with names that echo the political lingua franca—"choice" and "reproductive health." These are the nightmarish abortion mills where black and Hispanic women are dying at a rate 2 1/2 times that of white women; where doctors stop midway through a procedure to shake down patients for more cash and turn them out into the street bleeding if they can't pay up; where staff members seldom change the bloody sheets on the beds; where patients scream through their abortions with no anesthesia because administering painkillers is costly and risky. In an assembly line that performs as many as 90 abortions a day, there simply isn't time to take care of these problems.

Most abortion providers, one assumes, are reasonably competent, as they were even before 1973, when Planned Parenthood estimated that

> nine out of 10 illegal abortions were performed by qualified physicians. But, prior to Roe v. Wade, the fact that these doctors were often breaking the law also kept the number of abortions low—as few as 200,000 per year by some estimates—and effectively discouraged most doctors from taking unnecessary risks with their patients. Legalization removed these constraints. An unscrupulous abortion doctor could simply hang out his shingle, confident that he would be shielded by abortion-rights rhetoric that uniformly proclaims him a hero, even if his motive is not compassion but greed.[2]

The horrible facts

It's amazing to me that in spite of advanced medical technology and the availability of contraceptives, the United States has the highest abortion rate of any Western industrialized nation. We rank ninth worldwide. Abortion is now the most common surgical procedure in this country![3] It's a profitable business.

One baby loses its life every twenty seconds because of abortion. That's more than 4,300 babies aborted in the United States each day![4] How the line has moved! Life used to be precious; today some believe the unborn baby with a beating heart and full features is nothing less than a blob of tissue.

Listen to a conversation that took place several years ago when a ***Miami Herald*** reporter posed as a potential client in a Florida abortion clinic:

"What about the baby? I'm worried about hurting the baby," the reporter said to the clinic owner.

"What baby?" he answered. "There's just two [menstrual] periods there that will be cleared out."

"You mean I'm not pregnant?" the reporter asked.

"Oh, you're pregnant. But there is no baby there...two periods and some water," the owner said and then added: "If you don't terminate, then it will become a fetus, and after birth it will become a baby."[5]

Young women are being told these lies and are blind to the truth. A baby is not just "two periods and some water." It is a human being, a human life! That's a scientific fact!

Did you know that after just eighteen days of life the unborn baby's heart begins to beat? At forty days, brain waves can be recorded. In the sixth week, it will move when its lips are gently stroked. All twenty milk-teeth buds are present at six-and-a-half weeks.

At eight weeks, a baby whose nose is tickled will flex its head backwards. The infant may even attempt to suck its tiny thumb. An eleven-week-old fetus can swallow, and all body systems are working. By the next week, fingernails are visible. The child can hear by fourteen weeks. Then, at sixteen weeks, eyelashes are present. One week later, the baby can dream. By about eighteen or nineteen weeks, if a very bright light shines on a woman's abdomen, a baby's hand will slowly move to shield its eyes. It will cover its tiny ears in response to loud music!

This baby is alive, human, and complete.[6]

Abortion is a national tragedy. Yet, half of this nation's unmarried teen pregnancies end in abortion.[7]

Since 1973, America has lost a whole generation of young people. About 26.5 million babies have died because of abortion.

How did we ever arrive at the point that human beings would decide if children live or die? A few decades ago, Americans would have recoiled in horror at the mere suggestion a woman could legally end the life of her developing child.

But the line moved. Deciding to end a baby's life is now called a "choice," not a character deficit.

Character is the issue

Where did this character crisis come from? How can those who strongly protest cruelty to animals remain silent when mothers destroy their developing babies?

Consider this:

In the United States, legal abortion was generally unavailable until 1970, when a few states liberalized their laws. Early in 1973, the Supreme Court declared restrictive abortion laws unconstitutional because they "violated the woman's right of privacy." In two 1973 cases, *Roe v. Wade* and *Doe v. Bolton*, the Supreme Court struck down two state laws prohibiting abortion. The victory granted women in the United States as much right to have abortions during the first six months of pregnancy as any other minor surgical procedure. Supreme Court Justice Harry Andrew Blackmun wrote the opinion in these landmark cases, which held the right to privacy allowed a woman to decide whether or not she wanted to end her pregnancy. He declared a fetus was not considered to be a person under the U.S. Constitution and therefore was not entitled to a legal right to life.

Just who are "Roe" and "Doe"?

"Jane Roe" was a divorced Dallas bar waitress, and "Mary Doe," an Atlanta homemaker. Both women became pregnant, asked for abortions, and were turned down. The babies were born, and "Jane Roe" eventually put her two-year-old up for adoption. "Mary Doe" did the same with her son.

By the way, the word *fetus* is a Latin word. It means "offspring" or "young one."

Why abortion?

Why do women choose to have abortions? Listen to the reasons given by four teens.

Sandy enjoys life. She attends graduate school and has big career plans. She's afraid a baby would bring too much of a lifestyle change. She opts for an abortion.

Ruthie is in high school. She decides on an abortion because she can't afford to quit school and financially take care of herself and her child.

Kate wants to have a good time in the fast lane. She believes sexual activity is part of her lifestyle. She decides to abort her growing baby. She does not want the responsibility of a child.

Grace comes from a Catholic family. They believe she's still a virgin. She aborts her baby soon after discovering she is pregnant. She doesn't want her family to know she has been sexually intimate.

Most abortions are performed because women did not expect to become pregnant. In other words, they abort for the convenience of the mother, the father, or the families involved.

Some abortions are referred to as "designer abortions." They are performed because the couple wants to select their baby's gender. Can you believe one third of the medical geneticists in the United States are willing to order prenatal tests to determine a child's sex, even if it means the parents might abort a fetus that isn't the "right" sex! In most cases, these aborted babies are girls.[7]

How could the Supreme Court ever decide a person has "the right to do as an individual wishes"[8] when it means the death of a developing child?

Not long ago, when a pregnant woman shot herself in the pelvis and killed her unborn child, she was charged with manslaughter. In a recent auto accident, the driver was charged with manslaughter when a pregnant woman's unborn child died.

The Susan Smith case proved people in this society will not tolerate the killing of children. She strapped her two little boys into car seats and sent them plummeting to their deaths at the bottom of a lake in a driverless car. This enraged a nation, and she received a life prison sentence. But had she aborted those same small boys just one day prior to their births, she would have been protected by the Supreme Court and applauded by pro-choice organizations.

What about the unborn child? Does he or she have any rights in this country? Apparently not.

The decision to legalize abortion has embroiled this nation into a bitter moral battle. And abortion cases are rapidly increasing.

Important facts

Abortion is the termination of a pregnancy. A *spontaneous abortion*, or miscarriage, ends a pregnancy without human interference. But an induced abortion is a medical procedure. It requires a decision.

The public needs to know the truth about medically induced abortions and what happens to a baby when a pregnant woman, often a teenager, decides to abort medically.

Suction aspiration is the most common method used during early pregnancies. The abortionist first paralyzes the womb opening called the cervical muscle ring and then stretches, or dilates, it open. This is difficult because the cervix is hard or "green" and not ready to open. He inserts into the uterus a plastic tube with a knife-like edge on the tip. The suction traveling through this tube is similar to a vacuum cleaner but twenty-nine times more powerful. The force tears the baby's body into pieces. The doctor cuts the deeply rooted placenta from the inner wall of the uterus and uses the tube to suction the scraps out into a bottle.

A **D & E (dilation and evacuation)** abortion is performed after sixteen weeks. Using a sharp surgical instrument, the physician cuts the baby into small parts and then pulls out the pieces with forceps. He often has to crush the child's head to extract it.

Saline abortion is a procedure in which a salt solution is injected into the amniotic fluid surrounding the baby. This poisons the child and burns its skin. The baby is born dead. This child is called a "candy-apple" baby because of its skin color when burned to death by the solution.

A **hysterotomy** is performed in late pregnancy. The physician cuts the womb open, delivers the baby live, and allows it to die of exposure.[9]

In **partial-birth abortion**, the doctor usually extracts live brain tissue for research and treatment of conditions like Parkinson's Disease. The procedure is also performed for the convenience of the mother. It's last-minute birth control. The pregnant woman carries her child to at least twenty weeks or into the final stages of pregnancy. The live unborn baby is partially delivered feet first and killed with its head still in its mother's womb. In 1996, Congress passed legislation to ban partial-birth abortions, but President Bill Clinton vetoed the bill.

Devastating effects

People are misled into believing legal abortions are safe and contribute to the health of the mother. This is not true. Abortions may be legal, but they are often quite painful and not safe! They are not healthy.

Teenagers are at greater risk than more mature women. Why? The cervix of the young teenager, pregnant for the first time, is invariably small, tightly closed, and especially liable to damage when dilated. Physical and emotional damage from an abortion is greater in a young girl. In the case of a younger mother and an older fetus, the complication rate is higher. Teenagers often suffer from some of the most catastrophic complications, such as post-abortion syndrome.

Catherine Whitney's book, ***Whose Life***, describes a woman's inability to process the fear, anger, sadness, and guilt surrounding her abortion experience. It includes grief over the loss of her baby and lack of peace with God, herself, and others involved in the abortion decision.[10]

This syndrome affects vast numbers of women who have undergone an abortion. Symptoms include "deep depression, flashbacks of the abortion, crying jags, sleeplessness, nightmares.... It can lead to substance abuse, severe repression of all emotional expression, and even suicide. It doesn't necessarily happen right away, but it happens eventually.

Mom once served as a volunteer counselor at the local Sav-a-Life office. She told me about an affluent married woman she once counseled. The woman had two children, ages seven and nine, and was pregnant with a third. Her husband insisted she have an abortion. She told Mom how quickly the abortion people moved to abort her baby. They were rude to her, and the pain she felt throughout the procedure was intense. She suffered physically as well as emotionally. This woman would wake up at night to check the commode to look for signs of tissue from her baby. Mom eventually had to refer her to a professional counselor.

If a baby dies after birth, parents can see the dead child, hold him, give him a name, and make funeral arrangements. Visiting the grave can help with the healing process. Parents and the extended family can mourn. Recovery is never easy for parents who lose a baby they loved. They have memories to associate with the life, even if it was brief.

When parents lose a baby through abortion, there is no opportunity to mourn. They may feel a sense of loss but cannot properly grieve. They never saw the child, held it, named it, and have no good memories. There is usually no funeral. Most aborted babies are thrown away with the day's trash. And the parent is responsible for the death.

A teen is especially vulnerable to post-abortion syndrome, especially if she wants to keep the baby but is pressured into an abortion.

A woman who has had an abortion suffers many losses: the actual loss of the child as well as what might have been. She may dream about the aborted baby at night. When she sees other children, she may think about her aborted baby and wonder what the child would look like. Recovery is difficult, and this grief is hard to resolve. She may have lost a lover, a relationship, a potential marriage, the possibility of motherhood in the future, and her dreams and hopes for herself as well as her aborted child.

Some teens, like Margot, live with overwhelming guilt after the abortion. They acquire a self-hatred that follows them like a shadow. They may feel the need to punish themselves. Some mothers even cramp and vomit on the baby's due date.

"I have this little ghost now," Linda Francke admitted after her abortion. Mrs. Francke was a mother of three and just starting a career when she became pregnant. She and her husband agreed another baby would cause an unbearable strain.

"It certainly does make sense not to be having a baby right now," she remembers telling her husband. "We [said] that to each other all the time."

"But I have this little ghost now. A very little ghost that only appears when I'm seeing something beautiful, like the full moon on the ocean last weekend. And the baby waves at me and I wave at the baby."[12]

As one doctor writes: "It is easier to scrape the baby out of the mother's womb than to scrape the memory of the baby out of her mind."

How true.

Full circle

Whatever happened to "Jane Roe," the woman whose unwanted pregnancy led to the legalization of abortion in the United States?

Her real name is Norma McCorvey. She recently had a life-changing experience.

She told a reporter: "I think abortion is wrong. I think what I did with Roe v. Wade was wrong. And I just have to take a pro-life position on choice."

She asserted, "I'll be...helping women save their babies."

In 1989, Gannett News Service reported McCorvey's child

which she almost aborted had been located and was strongly pro-life.[13]

And Sue? Whatever happened to the staff member who worked for Dr. Clark, the abortionist?

After Mary's death, Sue left the abortion industry. She now operates a crisis pregnancy motor home which provides information, pregnancy testing, and ultra-sound facilities.

"I was challenged inside the abortion centers each time a woman saw her baby (by mistake) on a sonar. I watched her face change from hard to soft, and immediately she began to love and bond with her child and walked out of that office determined to give life to her baby."

Sue recalls her initial introduction to the abortion business. She regarded it as a job that helped women. But after witnessing her first abortion, all illusions disappeared.

"I had expected a clean, neat, sterile procedure where the women felt no pain and no suffering or crying. What I saw was a terrified young girl, screaming to the top of her lungs in pain, both mentally and physically, I saw a doctor that cared nothing for her, I saw a baby ripped apart. I leaned against the wall and felt as if I was going to pass out; I slid down the wall. I am not sure what happened to me, but I just went cold after that. I dehumanized the baby; I dehumanized the girl having the abortion; they meant nothing to me."[14]

Abortion is not an option, as far as I'm concerned. Terminating a fetus is killing a child. At the 1994 National Prayer Breakfast, 83-year-old Mother Teresa was undaunted by the presence of President Bill Clinton and Vice President Al Gore, who are pro-abortion. She proclaimed with confidence, "Any country that accepts abortion is not teaching its people to love, but to use any violence to get what they want." She received thundering applause for calling abortion "the greatest destroyer of peace today" and labeling the act "a direct killing of the innocent child."[15]

There's more!

Abortion is tragic, but it's not the only death-on-demand issue that we are facing in our culture. There's a new frontier—euthanasia. This practice, coming on the heels of abortion, was predicted by the philosopher Francis Schaeffer about twenty years ago. He suggested that once a society accepts abortion, it soon will rationalize euthanasia. The line is moving again. And it's heading toward physician-assisted suicide.

Dr. Jack Kevorkian is at the forefront of the debate. The courts in America are affirming the practices he pioneered. The Ninth Circuit Court of Appeals ruled the state's responsibility to protect life is not as important as an individual's right to privacy. Remember right to privacy from *Roe v. Wade*? Remember the more than one million abortions a year as a result of that ruling? Could something similar happen with physician-assisted suicide?

If the government does not feel compelled to protect a life, one day the government may feel a compelling interest to end it. Ponder the implications for older people who have high medical bills, need constant care, and have exhausted their resources. It may sound extreme to think about the government one day finding it convenient to use euthanasia to avoid dealing with issues surrounding old age. But millions of abortions also sounded extreme twenty-five years ago.

The idea of physician-assisted suicide and abortion is also disturbing to doctors who take the Hippocratic oath to preserve life. Hippocrates said, "To please no one will I prescribe a deadly drug, nor give advice which may cause death." He wrote this thousands of years ago, and his standards have endured for generations.

Physician-assisted suicide is legal in the Netherlands. In that nation in one year, doctors ordered lethal overdoses of pain medication in 8,100 cases. Of those, 61 percent of the patients did not consent to their deaths.[16]

It's unthinkable a physician could take part in killing people. There is a frightening potential for abuse in this practice. Tolerance of this practice would become a prescription for further chaos in our country. It poses a tremendous ethical dilemma if our society continues to move the line.

CHAPTER 5

The Best Option

Someone once asked what I would say if I wrote a letter to my biological mother. I thought for a long time:

What would I say?

How do I feel toward her?

How would I begin a letter to the woman who gave me life, someone I've never met?

Should I say, "Dear Mom" or "Dear Biological Mom"? I would feel awkward addressing her as "mom" or "mother" when I do not even know her name.

Perhaps I would write something like this:

Dear Precious Woman,

You did something I wish more women had the courage to do. You didn't terminate your pregnancy when it became uncomfortable or embarrassing to you. Because you are Italian, perhaps you grew up in a Catholic family, and abortion was not an option.

All I know is you decided to give me life. I don't know how you went through the pain of relinquishing me after going through labor and delivery. I had just come out of your body, and you didn't even get to hold me. But I know my adoptive mom and dad are really happy you gave them that opportunity. I really hope you later had other children to hold.

You'll never know how thankful I am for your decision. It is wonderful when teenage moms, like you, love their newborn babies as much as you loved me. You were very unselfish, courageous, and brave to give me up. Be assured that you did what was best for us both in the long-term.

I want you to know I love you deeply. I can't express how much I love you, though I've never seen you and probably never will. But please accept my gratitude. I thank you every time I stand before a teenage audience to speak. Every single time, I make that speech in your honor.

Love,
Amie Beth

Two gifts

My biological mother gave me two gifts. The first was the gift of life. I am so thankful she chose life over death for me.

The second was love. She expressed it by giving me to parents who would cherish and care for me.

Let me tell you about these wonderful people—my adoptive mother and father—Doug and Barbara Dickinson.

They met as students at Taylor University in Indiana in the mid-sixties. After graduation, they married and Doug went on to medical school while Barbara worked in microbiology. The marriage was strong, and the Dickinsons wanted to begin a family. They tried to have a child for many years without success.

Year after year, they endured multiple infertility tests which showed everything was normal. But conception never happened. So they poured themselves into their work. They made arrangements to do medical missions work in the Niger Republic. But a week before they were scheduled to leave,

Mom's doctor called with exciting news that would change their missions plans.

"Are you still interested in becoming parents?" he asked. Greeted with a hearty yes, he continued, "Well, a baby girl was born this morning and needs a good home."

Five days later, I went home with my new mom and dad. I immediately was the center of a celebration complete with grandparents, aunts, and uncles—an instant family—all welcoming me as the first little Dickinson.

We moved to Birmingham, Alabama, which would become my hometown, when I was six months old. Dad accepted a medical residency at the University of Alabama at Birmingham and then later set up practice in this city.

But our family didn't stop growing.

Fifteen months later, my parents adopted another newborn, my little brother, Christopher Douglas. I love Chip. We enjoy a wonderfully close relationship.

But the Dickinson family was not yet complete.

One day, while I was in the fifth grade, Mom asked. "How would you like a baby doll for Christmas?"

I reminded her I was a big fifth-grader and didn't play with dolls any more.

"No, Amie Beth," she said, "I mean a real baby doll! Your little sister was born today. I'm picking her up tomorrow." She knew this was an answer to my prayers. They named her Arden.

Chip and Arden Dickinson were two gifts given to our family by women who chose life for their babies instead of death. Because our family received these gifts made possible through adoption, I am painfully aware this is another area in which the line has moved.

Adoption used to be an honorable way for an unmarried young woman and her family to respond to an unwanted pregnancy. There was shame and social scorn attached to pregnancy out of wedlock. A pregnant girl often was not allowed to attend school in her hometown. Everyone understood that a girl who revealed that she was pregnant would be suspended from school—or possibly expelled.

As a result, if she did not marry the father, she might have to leave home and visit an out-of-town relative until the baby was born. Or, she would be admitted to a home for unwed mothers. She would receive prenatal care, the opportunity to continue with school, and counseling at the maternity home. An adoption would be arranged for the infant. In most cases, the birth mother realized she lacked the resources or desire to raise and support a child.

She would return to her hometown and enroll again in school after the birth. Most people hoped she had learned a strong lesson about what happens when you step across the line and engage in sexual activity outside of marriage. The consequences definitely deterred behavior beyond the line.

It's human nature to try to avoid the results of your actions. Particularly when they are severe. Today birth control and legal abortion are widely available. As a result, many people believe that sexual activity outside of marriage brings no ill effects.

Adoption, instead of being an honorable solution to the problem of unwanted pregnancy, was berated by some "enlightened" people as undesirable and psychologically damaging. They said this act of love inflicted emotional pain and caused suffering and therefore should be avoided. The way to avoid it, they said, was to get an abortion. Again, the line moved. What was honorable was painted as dishonorable, and what was dishonorable gained esteem.

The pain of infertility

There are many couples today, just like my parents, who desperately want a child but cannot produce a baby. Infertility brings tremendous pain. Many couples yearn for a chance to adopt. Unfortunately, the opportunities are limited.

I recently heard a very sad statistic. About 1.5 million abortions were performed in 1995—while 1.6 million couples had their names on adoption waiting lists.

How dare anyone say these unborn babies are unwanted!

They are desperately longed for by infertile couples. In fact, in the United States, infertility treatment has become a billion dollar industry. Infertility is not only emotionally painful but also expensive. High-tech in vitro fertilization treatments alone cost between $6,000 to $8,000 with a 50 percent pregnancy rate for patients under age 40.

Whys and hows of adoption

Babies and young children are a tremendous responsibility. They need constant care, day after day, year after year. Sometimes a teenage birth parent just isn't ready or able to nurture the child. Adoptive parents may be better able to provide a home for the child.

What exactly is adoption? It is a procedure in which a person becomes the legal parent of a child who is not his or her biological offspring. Adopted children have all the rights and duties of biological children. In the United States, adoptions can be handled privately or through public or private agencies.

Lifeline Children's Services, an organization in Birmingham, Alabama, arranges adoptions and challenges young women who are considering keeping their babies to ask themselves some important questions: "Am I able to give a child what it needs? Would I have to count on my parents to take over for me? Can I raise a child and meet my own needs? Finish school? Start a career? Am I really ready to become a good parent on my own?"

To pursue adoption, one or both birth parents usually contact an agency or attorney. If it's an agency, a social worker helps the young pregnant woman or couple consider the choices of marriage, single parenthood, or adoption. It is important that they make an informed decision. The social worker is equipped to also help with decisions about prenatal care, housing, finances, education, and other concerns.

The expectant mother should not be rushed into a decision. It's important to protect the birth parents' rights. When everyone is sure about the adoption, the social worker arranges for the necessary papers to be drawn up. The child cannot legally join a new family until an adoption agreement is signed or a court has terminated the birth parents' rights.

Can birth parents take part in choosing the adoptive parents? Yes, if they wish to do so. They usually have a range of choices in making an adoption plan for their child.

Adoption is a unique life experience for those involved. How do birth parents find out how the child is doing in the new family? The adoption agency or legal representative assists birth parents, adopted persons, and adoptive parents throughout their lifetimes as needed. A birth parent may request information anytime. Today, birth parents and adoptive parents are much more open about exchanging non-identifying information. Birth parents may want to know how the child is doing; and adoptive parents, or the adopted person, may desire more background information, particularly about medical records.

Christa Jones, a nineteen-year-old African-American college sophomore, considered abortion when she was four-and-one-half months pregnant but instead chose adoption for her baby girl.

"We spent two days together," remembers Christa about her daughter's birth. "On the third day, it was time to give her away.... She was asleep when I told her good-bye. And that was also the day I had to sign the adoption papers. It was the hardest thing I have ever had to do. I had to remind myself that I was doing this for her.... I made my choice. It was the one that I thought would be best for my baby and for me."

There has been a long-standing myth about adoption. It says a mother who really loves her baby can't give it up. This is untrue! Choosing adoption is a mature decision.

I was appalled by a comment by Jon Ryan of Concerned United Birthparents, when he said, "Adoption is worse than abortion. You're giving up your flesh and blood."

I'd like to tell Jon Ryan that adoption spells L-I-F-E, and abortion spells D-E-A-T-H. Adoption spells **L-O-V-E** in big, bold, capital letters! Young parents who put a baby up for adoption usually love the child. They are placing the baby's well-being before theirs. They may want to keep the child but cannot adequately provide. Giving a child to a couple who can is an unselfish and loving act.

The rest of the family

My little sister, Arden, is now thirteen years old. She's an angel. We share a unique relationship. I longed for a sister for more than six years before she was born. She is beginning to come into my bedroom now to read my magazines and use my hair spray. With our age difference, sometimes I feel like her mother instead of her sister. Sometimes the love and attention she shows me astonishes me. She's a neat little person, and I love her dearly.

My brother, Chip, just turned twenty-two, and we are very close. We went out to dinner last night. Just the two of us. And we discussed our love for our family and our meaningful childhood. Chip and I remembered how Dad would come home from work and hug us. If it was late, he'd tiptoe into our rooms and kiss us on the cheeks. He really loved us! Even though he was very busy in his medical practice, he always had time for us. And Mom, how she dedicated herself to us and sacrificed her own gifts and time to give us so many wonderful opportunities.

Long after the dishes had been cleared away and our bill paid, Chip and I sat at the table and talked into the night. We were able to do that because years ago, two women chose the best option.

CHAPTER 6

The Cost of Sex

What would it be like to lose your life because of a terrible disease? Is a few moments of sexual pleasure worth dying for? Dennis passed away from HIV complications just a short time after he spoke the following words from his hospital bed:

> Knowing that I'm not going to live to see the fulfillment of the hopes and dreams I've had is pretty hard to take. There's a lot of times I wake up and I cry in the middle of the night.... And there's a lot of times that I cry in the middle of the day. Knowing that I'm just going to die, and that I'm going to die a pretty painful and horrible death.
>
> A young life is far too great to throw away on one sexual experience or on a high or whatever. I mean it's just far too great. The safe sex condom campaign is simply a matter of continuing in promiscuity and continuing in sexual behavior that really is not safe.[1]

Human immunodeficiency virus (HIV) brings the death sentence of AIDS, technically called acquired immune deficiency syndrome. There is no known cure and none in sight. Researchers predict it will be ten to fifteen years before they find a cure.

HIV is no respecter of persons. It's not just a disease for homosexuals, prostitutes, or drug users or the promiscuous. The symptoms can be treated to prolong life, but eventually the patient dies from HIV complications or AIDS. It is a predictable, progressive disease.

HIV is spread by the exchange of body fluids between two people. The virus can live in a variety of body fluids: blood, semen, vaginal secretions, breast milk, saliva, tears, and urine. In some fluids, the virus exists in higher concentrations than others. HIV tampers with the immune system so a body can no longer fight off diseases.

No one knows the origin of HIV. Scientists have offered a number of explanations. Before 1977, it was almost unknown. Some believe one infected person, referred to as "Patient Zero," brought the virus to the United States around 1980. Others believe it has been around for some 300 years or longer. Until recently, they explain, world conditions were not ripe for it to be passed around. Over the last three decades, a tremendous increase in international travel and sexual activity with multiple partners has set the stage for its death march. Now the virus is spreading like wild fire in a vast dry forest.

HIV has become a global epidemic. According to 1996 statistics, 22 million people worldwide are HIV infected. The World Health Organization projects 40 million will be infected by the year 2000.

Consider some alarming statistics. In 1996, one out of 100 African-American women were infected, along with 1 out of 500 Caucasian women. The rate of infection is especially high in crowded inner-cities among black males under twenty years of age.[2] In 1993, HIV became the leading cause of death in the United States among persons ages 25-44.

Why the dramatic increase? Is it because many people think

the line has moved and they don't have to face the results of their actions? This shows up in their attitudes:

"Couldn't happen to me!" Teens think AIDS lurks somewhere in the shadows, waiting to attack only homosexuals, prostitutes, or drug users. They consider themselves untouchable.

"Abstinence? You're kidding!" There is a widespread belief, even among educators, that abstinence is not possible for young people. They say it's unrealistic. People see teens as hormone-driven with no control over their sexual behavior.

"I'll use a condom and have safe sex." Some teens actually believe condoms can protect them from HIV! They hear condoms are 98 percent effective. In reality, the figure is more like 78 percent in protecting against pregnancy and 69 percent in blocking the AIDS virus. HIV is 450 times smaller than sperm. Those are not the kind of odds on which you would stake your life!

Imagine your first experience in bungee jumping. There you stand, perched on the side of the Hell's Canyon Bridge. You have strapped cords to your ankles, and your waist harness is tight and secure. You can hardly wait to let go. Your heart rate doubles right before you leap, but the instructor adds, "You're going to have a great time. It'll be exciting! You'll never experience anything like it." But then he warns, "I have to mention something: The cord is strong and will probably keep you from falling to your death, but there is a 31 percent chance the cord will break. But, go ahead. It will be a wonderful experience."

Would you jump? Not for any amount of money! Condoms are like that bungee cord. There's a good chance a condom will prevent pregnancy and maybe even reduce your chances of catching a disease. But, then again, there's a good possibility it won't. If it doesn't and if that disease is AIDS, then, like the bungee jumper, you will fall to your death. There are no second chances.

So while the cute little condoms in the television ads are dancing around the bedroom and the government is encouraging their use, young people are becoming infected with HIV and dying of AIDS. In fact, HIV has already killed more people than the entire Vietnam War.

Russian roulette

I've heard about kids who play Russian roulette. A group passes around a revolver loaded with only one bullet. The idea is each kid spins the cylinder, then aims the muzzle at his head and pulls the trigger. The gun may fire, or it may not. It's a gamble. If it does go off, the kid pulling the trigger could die. Or he might blow away part of his brains and spend the rest of his life depending on family members for care. It is a reckless act, a stupid stunt.

Irresponsible sex is somewhat like Russian roulette. If you are having sexual intercourse, you have no way of knowing if the other person is infected with HIV. It's a risk. A partner might have the virus and not know it. It is most infectious long before it shows up on any test. Only one act of intercourse can change your life drastically. One sexual experience can inflict a death sentence, as well as years of agony, pain, and other horrible consequences.

If you beat the odds and do not become infected with HIV, you still run the risk of catching one or more of twenty-five sexually transmitted diseases.

A virus or bacteria doesn't discriminate. It doesn't check your ID. It doesn't know the difference between races. It strikes the rich, poor, and middle classes. Once a person becomes infected with a sexually transmitted disease, it is likely for life. Many organisms are becoming more and more resistant to treatment.

According to the Center for Disease Control, 2.5 million adolescents contract such a disease each year. Nationwide, about 1 million women become sterile annually because of sexually transmitted diseases. A disease that can cause infertility - chlamydia - effects more teens than any other age group. About a third of all sexually active teens are infected with this disease. "We could be bringing up a generation of infertile women," says Dr. Vicki Alexander, an authority on teenagers who are infected.[3]

In the fifties, sexually transmitted diseases were not a major threat. No one had ever heard of HIV or AIDS. Herpes was uncommon, and chlamydia was only a far-away germ that caused blindness in Africa. Of course, syphilis and gonorrhea had been around awhile. A person who contracted syphilis could be treated with a shot of penicillin. Other antibiotics cured gonorrhea.

Times have changed. And diseases have changed as well.

About one out of four sexually active teenagers, or approximately 2,000 teenagers a day, acquire sexually transmitted diseases. In addition to causing sterility, they can attack major body organs, increase the likelihood of tubal or ectopic pregnancies, and lead to cervical cancer, pelvic inflammatory disease, and death. Unborn babies can contract diseases from their infected mothers. In babies, sexually transmitted diseases cause blindness, infection, pneumonia, premature birth, mental retardation, and death.[4]

Every time people have sex, they are not just engaging in intercourse with their partners. They are having sex with every other person with whom their partners have ever had sex.

Teenagers face a 10 percent greater risk than adults of acquiring and being damaged by a sexually transmitted disease. Why?

A teenage girl's cervix has a lining which is less resistant to these germs.

She doesn't always ovulate during a menstrual cycle. As a result, a girl has a greater chance of infection because her cervical mucus is not as thick.

Teens are less resistant to infection because they have lower levels of antibodies in their systems.

Teenagers who start having sex at a young age have more sexual partners. The risk of catching a sexually transmitted diseases increases with the number of partners.[5]

Sexual mixing

We live in an age of sexual mixing. Joe S. McIlhaney, Jr., a Texas gynecologist, says, "It is common to see studies which show that sexually active teenagers have had five or ten sexual partners. Recently I had a 21-year-old girl tell me that she had 27 sexual partners before she decided that was not the type of lifestyle she wanted. As a result of this sexual mixing, there has been a progressive emergence of sexually transmitted diseases."[6]

Many teenagers are ashamed of their virginity because of peer pressure. Virginity has become sort of a curse, and they are embarrassed to admit they have not experienced sex.

The media promotes sexual promiscuity, and teenagers mimic what they see. Virginity is not popular on television's soaps, sitcoms, or talk shows. And kids watch a lot of TV. In fact, teenagers in the United States are exposed to about 14,000 sexual references and innuendoes on television annually.[7]

The media portrays sexual promiscuity as normal. It creates role models who often exhibit promiscuous behavior. Sexual activity before marriage and outside marriage is practiced by many movie, music, and television stars. They scorn sex within marriage as dull and boring. Their lifestyles communicate that sex outside of marriage is exciting, fun, and glamorous.

Doogie Howser M.D.

Do you remember the popular television show, "Doogie Howser, M.D."? Child prodigy Doogie, a fresh-faced kid with red hair and dimples, was an eighteen-year-old doctor. He was one of the most important people in the lives of hundreds of thousands of pajama-clad kids. They watched him religiously each Wednesday just before jumping into bed. He was their idol.

This enormously popular program began airing on ABC in the fall of 1989. As the series progressed, Doogie faced a problem his medical training just couldn't solve. In his words,

"Being a virgin is driving me nuts!" And so, on the fateful evening of September 25, 1991, Doogie and his girlfriend Wanda did something about it. The ratings skyrocketed.[8]

Unfortunately, television never shows what happens after young people become sexually active. It omits the broken hearts and fractured lives. It fails to mention unplanned pregnancies and overlooks the abortion that took the life of the unborn child. These shows never depict suffering due to sexually transmitted diseases!

Perhaps the episode following Doogie's sexual experience might go something like this:

Doogie Howser, HIV

Wanda and Doogie continued their sexual relationship for five or six more months. During this time, Doogie didn't realize he was carrying HIV. It was the result of accidentally being stuck by an infected needle when treating an AIDS patient. He was tested for HIV after the scary incident; but, in its early stages, the virus didn't show up. Doogie passed the virus to Wanda during sex.

In the meantime, something happened between Doogie and Wanda. Their relationship was no longer special. They never talked anymore, and sex had become the main purpose of their dates. Then Doogie spotted a new young nurse working in the emergency room. He became interested, and Nancy ended up in Doogie's bed.

Nancy was too cute for her own good. She had a regular boyfriend. Nancy and Jeff were sexually active. But Jeff also had another girlfriend, Sallye, and they, too, had sex.

Doogie had no symptoms of HIV, but Wanda lost weight, felt unusually tired, and had fever, diarrhea, and swollen glands. Doogie urged Wanda to get tested. She tested positive for the virus. Later, Jeff and Sallye also tested HIV positive.

Five, six, seven, maybe ten years down the road, Doogie will no longer be a fresh-faced kid with red hair and dimples. He will be no more than a skeleton covered with flesh, weak and dying in the final stages of AIDS. Wanda died of AIDS in just seven years. Before she died, she weighed only sixty-five pounds, half what she weighed when she first had sex with Doogie.

And what about Nancy? She was fortunate. She did not contract HIV. No one knows why. She just didn't. She somehow missed the Russian roulette bullet. But Nancy has her problems, too. During her many sexual contacts, she contracted chlamydia, one of the most common sexually transmitted diseases in the United States. She was one of 3 to 4 million people who suffer from chlamydia every year. She had no symptoms of the disease until the infection spread to her reproductive organs causing pelvic inflammatory disease. It was extremely painful and scarred her internally. As a result, Nancy became infertile. But, she's fortunate she's alive. That same year, some nine hundred other women died from pelvic infection. End of program!

Is a few moments of sexual pleasure worth this risk?

HIV and chlamydia are just two sexually transmitted diseases which infect teens. Another is human papilloma virus. Once rare, it is the one most likely to infect teens. About 38 percent of sexually active females ages thirteen to twenty-one have this disease. This is because condoms provide "virtually" no protection against the human papilloma virus. It is the most common medical problem seen by gynecologists and causes nearly all cervical cancers in America. They also experience venereal warts and painful intercourse. Males can contract these warts or develop cancer in their penises. One and a half million new cases of human papilloma virus appear each year.

Some 500,000 new herpes diagnoses are made annually. Did you know 20 million Americans suffer from this disease? For a person with herpes, future sexual experiences may be painful rather than joyful. Each year, there are one million new cases of pelvic inflammatory disease; 1.4 million people contract gonorrhea; and 300,000, hepatitis B. Syphilis is becoming resistant to antibiotics and is at a forty-year high with more than 130,000 new infections per year.[9]

What about you?

Perhaps you are a teen or you know teens walking dangerously close to the line and about to step over into a pattern of bad character choices. They will endanger their health, future reproductive capability, as well as their lives. What do you need to know? What can you tell them?

- Stop playing Russian roulette with your life. It's valuable. You are needed. You and your friends are the doctors, lawyers, decision-makers, caretakers, mothers, and fathers of the future. You are too important to allow your life to be snuffed out in adolescence.
- Read some truthful books and articles about sexually transmitted diseases. It's very possible you are receiving false information about this subject. Many people are confused. You need to know the truth about irresponsible, high-risk lifestyles.
- You can change your sexual behavior. Resolve to stand firm in your beliefs in the midst of sexually active peers. Seek out friends who have similar convictions.
- Realize sexually transmitted diseases don't just infect homosexuals, prostitutes, and drug users. You can be infected, too. In fact, the odds are good you will be infected unless you take control of your life now.
- Remember you are not like an alley cat in heat. You do have a choice about irresponsible sex.
- Make sure you have the correct information about condoms. You have probably heard you can have "safer sex" if you use condoms properly. Find out the truth.

Remember what Dennis said at the beginning of this chapter? "Knowing that I'm not going to live to see the fulfillment of the hopes and dreams I've had is pretty hard to take...."

Fortunately, HIV and sexually transmitted diseases are 100 percent preventable! In fact, they could be wiped out completely if people would just change their behavior. You do not have to live with these painful diseases. Nor do you need to die an agonizing death. There is a wonderful alternative! You can find it when you know where to draw the line in your life.

CHAPTER 7

Why Virginity?

What really happens when a teenager has sex? I'll tell you a true story. Leslie, an eighteen-year-old, described her experience this way:

> I always felt that I didn't want to have sex before I got married. When I became engaged, my fiancee and I kissed and did a lot of heavy petting but never went all the way. Then my sister asked me if we were having sex. She said that she and her husband did before they got married. She made it seem so exciting and off limits.
>
> Then the thought came, "If my sister did it, why can't I?"
>
> I convinced myself that it was okay because we were getting married. When we finally had sex I was tense, uncomfortable and guilty. It was a let-down and not at all how I had expected it to be. Instead of tenderness, we were in a hurry. Instead of love, there was guilt. I cried. All I could think about was that I wasn't a virgin anymore. I wanted our wedding night to be so special. I felt dirty, and even though I was going along with it

> as much as he was, I felt used. I lost respect for myself and for him. I felt that just by looking at me other people knew what had happened.
>
> There was a loss of innocence, not in a beautiful way, but in an ugly way. I still feel the pain and regret of what I did.[1]

"I still feel the pain and regret..."

I've heard other unmarried girls talk about their pain and regret in giving up their virginity. It reminds me of the following words I found in a brochure:

> Thousands of teenagers who said "yes" [to premature sex] will tell you they wish they had waited. Even if you don't get a disease or get pregnant, you can still get hurt. Breaking up with someone after you've had sex feels twice as bad. ...Maybe you think your friends will say you're cool if you have sex. Well, just wait until you catch a sexually transmitted disease. Every year, thousands of teenagers do. And the sex that was supposed to make them so popular, turns them into the school's biggest outcasts overnight.[2]

I recently asked a group of college women to answer these questions: *If you have been sexually active, why did you decide to engage in sexual intercourse? Have you ever ended a relationship with someone with whom you were sexually active? How did you feel?*

Here are some of their responses:

"I thought I was in love and ready emotionally."

"I was in love and in a three-year relationship. When we broke up, I was emotionally crushed. It's been three years, and it still hurts. You have sex, and when you break up, you don't get your whole self back."

"The first time I had sex, I was drunk. After that, I felt like 'you've already done it so why not again'? I feel badly we're not together anymore."

"I was pressured to have sex by a drunk guy in a pickup truck. Afterwards I felt cheap, used, degraded! Sick!!!"

"I had sex because I thought I loved him. But I broke up when he hit me."

"I felt I was in love and thought he loved me! Then I felt used, like I gave him something so special for no reason at all."

"I was stupid and thought the guy liked me. I thought sex was the only way to prove I loved him."

"I thought I was going to marry the person, but now everything has changed. I feel I have let down my future husband. Like there's a part of me he will never get. I don't know what love is. But I do wish someone would tell me!"

"I feel used. Premarital sex hurt me emotionally. If you love one another, you wouldn't want to hurt each other by having sex."

"I was drunk." (Alcohol is involved in many first-time sexual experiences.)

"I felt having sex was the only way to hold onto him. Since we've broken up, I feel I now have a second chance to change my future."

"We were planning to get married but couldn't due to finances. We had been dating two years and I thought we would be together forever. Now I feel hurt, terrible, dirty. I wish I hadn't had sex."

"I had sex for stupid, stupid reasons! Mainly ignorance! When we broke up, I wanted to die."

"I thought we were in love and sex would bring us closer together. HA!"

"I knew it was wrong but didn't understand why. I loved him, he loved me so I thought it was okay. When I finally understood why it was wrong, it was too late. Two years have passed since the relationship broke up, and it still hurts. I feel cheap, lost, naive, and taken advantage of. If it's love, and not lust, and if the guy really loves the girl, he can wait until they are married."

"The first time, I thought I had to have sex to keep him.

What a crock! I said 'no' the whole time, but he was too strong. The second time was with a former boyfriend who I confided in. After finding out I had had sex with the first guy, he got jealous and raped me. Is it wrong to hate him?"

"I was really in love with my boyfriend and he was an alcoholic. I showed him through sex I cared. Anyway, I was afraid he'd beat me or I'd lose him if I didn't. When we broke up and I started to college, I felt torn. Like half of me was missing."

"I had sex because of peer pressure in my first year of college. I was dating a much older guy who didn't share my same beliefs. I felt hurt when we broke up because I had done something I never intended to happen."

"I had sex because I believed I was in love, but I was wrong. When we broke up, I felt awful. I felt like an object, not a person. I lost my identity. I wish I had waited."

As I stated, these responses came from females. I'm not saying that males were the only ones at fault. In most cases, the females were willing participants. In some, they could have been the instigators.

When I go into high schools and colleges and speak to young people, they always ask the same question: "Why isn't anyone else telling us about the benefits of abstinence?"

Not an ice queen

As I talk about this subject, I want to make one thing perfectly clear. I'm not asking anyone to refrain from doing anything I'm not refraining from myself.

But I understand temptation. I'm not an "ice queen." I'm human like everyone else. The fact that I'm a virgin doesn't mean at age twenty-four I have not been sexually tempted. I have really enjoyed dating and I have gone out with a lot of different guys. We have had great times, but we have not had sex. The guys have known I would never pressure them or be pressured into any sexual situation.

I made a decision some years ago that I would save my virginity for the man I'll marry. I'm not saying it is easy. It's not! But I can honestly tell everyone abstinence is possible! I know firsthand the wonderful benefits of remaining a virgin until marriage. I am happy to wait for my first sexual experience within the special context of marriage.

If you're a teen, I urge you also to wait. There are many reasons why this is very important. I'll list them again. You can avoid unplanned pregnancies, sexually transmitted diseases, torn emotions, and broken hearts, and even death.

Without sex, a girl on a date can gain a good friendship and lose the possibility of being used. Trust me on this one.

This idea is by no means original with me. Throughout recorded history, in most civilized cultures, people have conducted their sexual relationships within the context of marriage.

Sexual behavior is rarely isolated from other moral issues in a person's life. Early intercourse goes hand in hand with other potentially health-endangering practices such as alcohol consumption, drug use, and smoking. The same kids who have premature sex are more likely to break the law and get in trouble at school. All of these actions have a common core: the absence of good character.

The stressful years

A large number of teens I talk to become sexually involved at young ages. Thirty years ago, when my mom and dad were teenagers, abstinence was just understood. People usually waited until marriage to have their first sexual experiences. If they didn't wait, they were secretive about it. Back then, young people did not openly discuss their sexual behavior and certainly didn't brag about losing their virginity!

But the line has moved. Today, only 10 percent of women who marry still possess their virginity, compared to 43 percent in the late sixties.[3]

There's no doubt about it, growing up today isn't like growing up thirty years ago. The Cleavers of "Leave it to Beaver" fame definitely don't live in today's average neighborhood! Childhood and the teenage years aren't easy now. They are highly stressful.

As I said before, teens are looking for intimacy and genuine friends who approve of them and love them for who they are.

Some have sex because they crave this so-called "intimacy." When a girl tells me she had sex in order to keep a boyfriend, I tell her premarital intercourse breaks up relationships faster than it strengthens them. Couples who have sex prematurely tend to communicate only physically. They seldom grow in their ability to communicate on intellectual, social, emotional, and moral levels. Experts tell me divorce and adultery are more common among couples who have had premarital intercourse. If sexual self control is impossible prior to marriage, then marital fidelity is more difficult after marriage.

I often tell a girl if she has to have sex with a boyfriend in order to keep him, he's not worth keeping. When a boy truly loves a girl, he will not ask her to give up her virginity. If he intends sex to be part of the relationship, he is experiencing lust, not love.

Kay Cole James is Virginia's Secretary of Health and Human Resources. On a recent visit with a group of high-risk ten- to fourteen-year-old girls, she asked, "Those of you who are sexually active, is it because you want to be ... ?

She continued: "If you are sexually active, are you enjoying it?"

They clearly answered no to both questions. So she said, "Let me get this right—you're risking your life and risking creating another life for something you don't want to do and that you don't enjoy?"[4]

The truth about condoms

Questaleicia Steemer is eighteen and already the mother of two-year-old twin boys.

She states raising children "is something I never thought I'd be doing in a million years." Then she adds: "When my babies turn eleven, I'm going to buy a box of condoms and say, 'Here they are. If you need them, use them.'"[5]

How sad that the Questaleicia Steemers in our society believe condoms prevent pregnancy!

We need one clear, concise message.

Of course, many don't want to hear the benefits and freedoms of abstinence. But when I have an opportunity to tell the problems associated with the 'safer sex' myth, students are ready to listen.

This message is usually not presented in schools.

Condoms are not working! The message of "safer sex" provides the sexually active with a false sense of security and encourages unhealthy behavior. It basically says:

• It's OK to have sex using a condom, even outside of marriage. It's perfectly normal, so go ahead and do it.

• Safer sex is perfectly achievable; a condom can protect you from pregnancy and disease.

• There are no such things as damaged emotions.

All of these statements are untrue and damaging!

It's unproductive to explain the benefits of self-control and then add, "But if you decide to have sex, remember to protect yourself." This statement undermines anything said about abstinence and its advantages. The average person will only remember the information after the word *but*.

Do condoms really allow a person to have safer sex, and what does that term mean anyway? Safer than what? In light of HIV, how safe is safe? Remember, condoms only cover a limited area and then don't protect either partner totally. Organisms present on exposed areas can be freely transmitted to the other person.

Medical evidence demonstrates there is no safe sex outside of a lifelong, mutually monogamous, committed relationship. People are gambling their lives on a thin layer of latex with a high failure rate!

Teens tell me they would rather learn how to say no to sex

outside marriage than to be taught how to use a condom.

The proper use of a condom reduces pregnancy risk. But please remember a condom will often not stop human papilloma virus and chlamydia, the two sexually transmitted diseases most likely to infect teens. Condoms also may leak, slip, or break.

Suppose you make airline reservations to fly to Denver. You board the plane, smile at the flight attendant, and find your seat. After you buckle your seat belt, the pilot greets passengers over the intercom:

"Good morning, folks. It's going to be a nice day for flying. The weather is great all the way to Denver. So just sit back and relax and leave the flying to us."

But as the plane taxies down the runway, he makes another announcement.

"We'll be taking off in just a few moments. Before we do, let me mention one small detail. We're having a few problems with the engines. While the airplane manufacturer tried to make the engines 100 percent safe, they were allowed a small margin of error in each motor. I can't guarantee you we'll get you to Denver safely. With these particular engines, I must advise you, we have a 31 percent chance of crashing somewhere near Des Moines."

Would you stay on that plane knowing you had almost a one in three chance of crashing and dying?

This imaginary example may help you put sexual risk in perspective.

I've already stated latex condoms are imperfect. They acquire holes about five microns in size during manufacturing.[6] Some viruses and bacteria are small enough to pass through these holes.[7]

The smallest detectable hole in a condom is one micron. But the human immunodeficiency virus is one-tenth to one-third the size of a micron.

Suppose I give you a tennis racket and I throw BBs at you. Your job is to catch the BBs with the racket.

The BBs are smaller than the grid strings of the racket and

will pass right through its holes. Dr. Robert Redfield, head of urology at Walter Reed Institute, said, "Trying to stop the HIV virus with a latex condom is like trying to catch a BB with a tennis racquet."

That's what happens when a condom is used. The tiny HIV virus goes right through the holes in the condom. A sperm which can pass through a condom is 500 times larger than the HIV virus!

At least half of Americans will be infected with a sexually transmitted disease by their thirtieth birthday.

What is the answer?

Several years ago, the surgeon general of the United States Public Health Service, Dr. C. Everett Koop, stated, "If you're young and you haven't yet achieved a mutually faithful monogamous relationship...then you should by all means *take the best possible precautions against disease by abstaining*. Period. That is my advice...and I don't think there's any better advice you can give."[8]

Some people have the audacity to say abstinence is a white, upper-middle-class value. They believe inner-city kids or "kids of color" can't control themselves. That's ridiculous. Even when people are bombarded with sexual messages and given wrong and conflicting information about sex, they can still practice abstinence.

Thomas Lickona said it well when he listed some benefits:

> 1. The only real, safe sex is having sex only with your marriage partner who is having sex only with you.
>
> 2. Abstinence offers freedom from guilt, doubt, and worry; sexually transmitted disease; pregnancy; the trauma of abortion; loss of reputation; and pressure to marry early.
>
> 3. Abstinence offers freedom to become more creative in sharing feelings, develop skills and

> abilities, develop healthy self-appreciation, achieve financial stability before having a family, and develop greater trust in marriage.[9]

I recently read a brochure that made some important points, which I'd like you to consider.

Most girls who begin to have sex are really looking for a good relationship. Building one takes time. Together you share with each other from your hearts so you get to know a person's beliefs, feelings, and thoughts. This develops mutual respect. Adding sex to that mixture doesn't speed it along. You can be sure that any guy who says, "The way to show you care about me is to have sex with me," is out to use you. That line has been around for generations.

There are better ways to let dates know you like them or love them. But sex is not one of those ways. Learn to be creative in expressing how you feel. Show you care with small acts of kindness and verbal expressions of affection. These never go out of style. One of the best ways to say you love someone is to refuse to participate in destructive behavior.

Let's say you are very grateful to a date who has been nice to you, and you want to repay the kindness. A simple, sincere "thank you" is enough. Sex should never enter into your expression of gratitude. Don't move the line.

Sexual control and marriage

It's popular in some circles for couples to live together before marriage. They say they want to experience a trial run. This arrangement seldom works. One reason is that engagements don't always end in marriage. After these relationships end, both women and men often complain of "feeling used." When the couples marry, the relationships have a high failure rate.

It's a fact: couples who experience sex before marriage have a 60 percent higher divorce rate than those who come to their wedding nights as virgins.[10]

Sexual self-control before marriage leads to marital fulfillment in the future. What can you expect to gain by waiting until marriage to experience sex?

A better understanding of sex within marriage. When a couple is committed to sexual abstinence, they take their marriage vows more seriously.

Absence of guilt, fear, and shame. People feel guilty when they do things they know are wrong. Teens know when they have lowered their code of conduct. They fear pregnancy, disease, and rejection. They also feel shame when the consequences of their actions catch up with them. People with self-control before marriage have no sexual baggage from past relationships or one-night stands to deal with after marriage.

Greater trust within marriage. Inappropriate sexual activity can become a habit and continue after the marriage vows are spoken. Would you trust a person who lacked self-control before marriage?

No comparison with former sex partners. Premarital sex leaves memories of former partners. Memories may fade with time, but they may not disappear completely. Once married, a person may unintentionally compare the spouse with former partners. This comparison can damage the marriage.

If at first you don't succeed...

Perhaps you've already had your first sexual experience. You *can change* your current sexual habits. It's called "secondary virginity."

"After having been sexually active, it is possible to regain the advantages of abstinence," says Maureen Duran in "Reasonable Reasons to Wait. "Decide to change; forgive yourself and others; change old habits; and develop ways of sharing that do not include sexual activity."[11]

A person who has had one or two cigarettes isn't a chain

smoker yet. Taking one or two drinks doesn't immediately classify the partaker as an alcoholic. It's possible to stop unhealthy behavior and regain self-control in these areas, as well as with sex. This may not be easy, especially when a boyfriend or girlfriend expects this activity. But anyone can do it. It's possible to enjoy all the freedoms of self-control. Kids who have been sexually active can start again. But how does someone do that?

You can make a decision to enjoy a new beginning. Here are some tips:

- Avoid situations that steer you the wrong way.
- Detach yourself from persons who cause you to slip.
- Know that dating and drinking do not mix.
- Avoid sexually stimulating TV shows, movies, and magazines.
- Seek support from friends and family members who share your ideas.
- Use your energy to develop new interests and hobbies.
- Accept what has happened in the past and learn from it.
- Develop non-physical ways of showing affection.
- Develop friendships.
- Decide to stand up for your decisions.[12]

You may not hear a lot about the positive value of abstinence before marriage. But it works. It has worked for me and for many people I know. There is a time and a place for sex—good sex, enjoyable sex, frequent sex—after marriage. There's no better time than now to decide that you will set this as your ideal.

CHAPTER 8

Closer To Home

Karen, home early from work, walked into her house and immediately noticed the silence. It was unusual. On most days, the blaring TV or stereo assured her that 15-year-old Genna was lounging in the den.

"Genna, honey, I'm home," she called.

Only silence greeted her.

Louder, this time. "Genna, where are you?"

No answer.

Alarmed, Karen hurried to the kitchen. A quick glance revealed that Genna had arrived home from school. A trail of books, sweater, and shoes led from the garage door to the refrigerator. Dirty dishes littered the table. "That's strange," she muttered when she saw two plates and two glasses, still filled with ice. But no Genna.

Karen climbed the stairs, wondering where her daughter might be. Genna had instructions not to leave home after school. But Genna wasn't expecting her mom this early.

Karen stopped at the top of the stairs when she saw Genna's door was closed. She nudged it quietly, thinking her child might be asleep. Her maternal gasp turned into a scream when she saw Genna in bed with a boy. No book on parenting had prepared her for this moment.

After a few seconds, a boy she barely knew emerged from the bedding and ran past her, taking a sheet with him.

Karen collapsed on the floor, sobbing from the depth of her being. Rage next colored her voice. "What's going on?" she finally choked out. "Who was that? What was he doing here?"

Genna was silent.

"Come out and face me!" Her ashen-faced daughter peeked out of the covers and whispered, "I love him, Mom. I didn't mean to hurt you."

"What do you mean you love him?"

Slowly it dawned on Karen this was not an isolated incident in which a male guest had forced his way on her naive daughter. The boy and her daughter were mutually involved in a sexual act.

Over the next few days, she learned her daughter and Philip had been sexually active for three months, and Genna was on birth-control pills.

It took Karen days before she could maintain her composure enough to discuss the incident with her sullen daughter who was now grounded. And she became more shocked by Genna's attitude.

"Why did you start having sex," she finally asked.

"Because I wanted to. I love him."

"But you know it's wrong."

"No, it's not wrong," answered Genna. "I love him, and he loves me."

"You're not married!" Karen reminded

"So? What does that have to do with it?" replied Genna.

"It has everything to do with it. Sex before marriage is WRONG!"

"Says who?"

"I say so, and that settles it."

"But what about you and Dad? Now that you're divorced, you both date. He sleeps around. I know it. You don't have to be a rocket scientist to figure that out. And what about the last guy you dated? He was here one morning when I came home from spending the night at Mallory's "

"But we're talking about you, Genna. You're young. You could get pregnant—or something worse. I love you and want to protect you."

"He loves me, too. And if we love each other, it's OK."

This is where they hit an impasse. Karen had a sick feeling. Her own behavior had blunted the values she wanted her daughter to know and live by. Genna had drawn a line all right—in the wrong place. And it was a line pointing toward disaster.

Learning to draw

There are some things I need to say to parents about the kind of home they provide, the kind of examples they set, and specifics of what to teach about sex-related subjects.

If you're a teen, feel free to read this chapter, learn from it and share it with your mom and dad. But it's mainly for them.Have you ever watched a small child trying to use a crayon for the first time? Someone usually has to help. Their eyes light up when they realize they can draw a line on a piece of paper.

My mom used to help me. She would place my fingers around the crayon and guide my hand to make those first marks. Soon I was saying, like all children, "I wanna do it myself!"

It didn't take me long to realize I could draw a line without my mom holding my fingers. Then those lines emerged into entire pictures.

It's been that way for me in many areas of life. My mom and dad taught me what to do. That's not unusual. Parents are supposed to do that.

Parents start teaching their young children by helping their little hands draw crayon lines. Later, they need to be there, to show them how to draw the permanent lines regarding character issues.

The starting point

Because of the sexual revolution that exploded in the sixties, many young people are facing the same kind of devastating situations as my birth mother. I see so many teenagers living with problems, pressures, and messed-up lives. They are suffering physically, emotionally, and morally. What are kids looking for? As I've said before, I believe they are desperately searching for intimacy.

This is a hard time to be a teen. The line between right and wrong, truth and lies, good character and bad character seems to be mobile, even erasable. Many people believe you can draw the line where you want to.

Where are the moral basics? What about the character crisis? Senator Daniel Coats says character "is a leading indicator of our future as a culture." Sadly, developing and maintaining good character isn't a priority with many people.

Society often portrays teens as containers of raging hormones they are unable to control. But I see teenagers in a different light. They have a God-given ability to make good decisions and use self-control. Teens can think and reason; they can be taught right from wrong. They can see the benefits of remaining sexually pure and understand the meaning of genuine love. It starts in the home.

Marriage today

Society today no longer values marriage. The media portrays life after the wedding as restrictive and confining. Society values individualism, choice, and unlimited personal liberty. "Till death do us part" has been replaced with "as long as I am happy." Courts promote divorce counseling instead of marriage counseling. Widespread divorces have created terrible emotional, financial, and spiritual problems for children.

Many people seem unwilling to totally invest themselves as husbands and wives. The result is marital unhappiness. Only a minority of children today are likely to grow up with both mother and father. Those from broken homes are less likely to form their own stable marriages.

D. James Kennedy says in ***Your Prodigal Child***, "Statistics show that children often repeat a parent's life pattern. Women who become pregnant out of wedlock find, more often than not, that their daughters repeat their mistake. The children of alcoholics have a greater likelihood of becoming alcoholics. Children whose parents are divorced are more likely to divorce. Young people who suffered sexual and physical abuse from their parents too often end up committing the same abhorrent crimes against their children."[1]

In marriage when commitment and faithfulness decline, children's well-being decreases. Marital failure is the common denominator behind teen pregnancy and other adolescent problems. Never before has one generation of American teenagers been less healthy, less cared for, or less prepared for life.

Marriage is society's most important vehicle for protecting children and turning them into good citizens.

Starting young

In your home, character education starts from day one at birth. Children observe how a father and mother treat each other. As a little girl, I watched my parents. My father always treated my mother with great respect, both as a person and as a homemaker and mother. My mother treated my father with respect and honor. They disagreed at times, as all married couples do, but I always knew they truly loved each other.

Their faithfulness to each other spoke volumes to me, my sister, and brother. They were dedicated to each other and to our family. They put our interests and needs first. They still share a love that is unconditional and doesn't fluctuate with various situations. I have learned from my parents how the opposite sex should relate to one another.

It's tragic America's families are so fragmented. Spousal abuse has become epidemic. Children no longer see their parents' respect and love for each other. I am grateful my parents have been, and continue to be, good role models for me.

How can parents discourage their children from sexual activity? By reinforcing the values and benefits of marriage! Here are some issues you need to address:

First, emphasize the moral relationship between love and sex. This is basic and important. Next, teach them that sexual misbehavior is the heart of the problem, not pregnancy and sexually transmitted disease. These are simply the effects. Then, communicate *it is possible* to enjoy the beauty of responsible healthy sexual behavior—within a permanent, monogamous, faithful relationship known throughout the ages as *marriage*.

Your children need to hear from you that sexual abstinence before marriage is the only safe way to prevent pregnancy, disease, abortion, and torn emotions. It not only reduces risks; it also eliminates them.

Stepping stones

It's difficult to raise children who reach adulthood with self-discipline, mature behavior, and good values! Yet, good character is the most important lesson a family, community, or a nation can teach.

Some values differ from culture to culture and family to family. But there are core values that have been the foundations of cultures and families for thousands of years. For example, the moral principles outlined in the Ten Commandments transcend cultures and are even respected by people who do not embrace other aspects of Judeo-Christian tradition. There is a line between right and wrong. But people don't just tune into good morals automatically at some magic age of maturity.

"Parents wouldn't expect their kids to suddenly become proficient at calculus without having first taken algebra and other math courses," says Bob Gorman. "They wouldn't expect them to make the varsity basketball team without having them play in youth leagues and middle school. Yet many parents make little effort to prepare their children to successfully navigate the teenage years, a period of time in which society envelopes teenagers in sexually explicit movies, videos and music."[2]

If a child is to learn right from wrong, you as a parent must be the primary teacher. This should be simple, but it is not. During the past three decades, society has drastically changed. We live in a culture that promotes "safer sex" among adolescents, hands out contraceptives and condoms in public schools, and inundates even preschoolers with sexual messages in the media.

Parents who teach values and good character habits and promote sexual abstinence before marriage seem like oddballs. They are in a minority but are the hope of our nation. It's an upstream swim for those who try to bring up children with good character and high morals.

Civilization, as we know it, cannot survive in a valueless and morally degenerate society. The solution to adolescent social problems begins with early education in the home.

Some parents don't know their kids' whereabouts or who their friends are. The character traits of friends can be the very character traits of the people they choose to marry. That's why you need to take an active role in their selection. Did you know that a teen's "sexual debut" often occurs at home after school—between 2 and 6 PM?

You must be a leader and not just your children's pals. Your role is to be the primary authority in your home and the loving enforcers of family rules. Kids have to be taught respect for authority and that bad behavior and irresponsibility bring negative consequences. You should monitor their schedules and activities.

Take the time and effort to know what your children are doing.

Kids want to know right from wrong and need boundaries.

A firmly placed line is important. They don't plan to have their first sexual experience at home in the afternoon. But this will happen when kids have hours of unsupervised time, are free to entertain friends of the opposite sex at home alone, and believe it's OK to have "safer sex"!

My brother, sister, and I were fortunate to have caring parents. They loved us and nurtured us in an incredible way. I realize now they sometimes had to make tough decisions about our upbringing. Because kids will be kids, there were times when we didn't like or agree with their decisions. But we knew where the line was. And I'm grateful.

Can we change?

As I look around at parents bringing children up today, I see disturbing things.

Some parents throw dollars into activities for their kids instead of spending time with them. This leaves them little opportunity to teach values and attitudes.

They have grown up as part of the "me" generation. Their own social lives and pleasures come before family time. Children seem to be a hindrance to them. They don't enjoy being around them. These parents demonstrate an attitude which says, "Soccer practice was my expenditure for you this week. Your Dad and I need to have `our' time this weekend, so we'll get a baby-sitter."

Be willing to say "no" when you feel uncomfortable about an activity or believe it is out-and-out wrong. There are many ways to say no. My Mom had a way of doing it without actually using the word. If I was invited to a party and she had questions about the invitation, she would say, "Oh, I'm so sorry. We're going to Nana and Grandpa's house that weekend." And then we'd go. By doing this, I didn't get the feeling she was saying no to my every request. She was able to save the big no for occasions which called for it. And some did.

Let your kids see you resisting peer pressure. Some parents

are just as vulnerable to it as kids. So many want their kids to be liked and accepted above all else. As a result, they are unwilling to stand up to their children. They crumble when a daughter says, "Well, Kim has a bathing suit like this" implying there's nothing wrong with it. Or, they allow their children to go to parties without ever investigating what will take place. Only later do they discover that the host parents were out of town. Or perhaps their son "John" didn't spend the night with "Brent" after all. Instead, the two went to "Eric's" house where there was no curfew.

Dear parents, I know it is hard, but the bottom line is, take time to investigate and invest in your children's activities.

There are a number of things you can do together as a family:

Worship together. This is important in itself but also has hidden benefits in developing character in every family member. You experience things together that you can talk about later over the dinner table or while riding in the car. Many issues you confront at church are stepping stones toward sound values.

Give as a family. Decide on a project you can do together. It may be something local, like working in a soup kitchen. In my city, various groups come together on Thanksgiving morning to feed breakfast to homeless people. Families prepare food at home and then take it downtown where they help serve it. Then they return home to enjoy their own feast.

Other families in my city open their homes for a weekend around Christmastime to young guests from a ranch for troubled youth.

There are other ideas. You could hold a family garage sale and give the proceeds to charity.

Or, there are things you could do outside your community. Some families go out of town together in order to participate in a building project—perhaps a church, school, or home in a needy community. If you explore the options, you will find something meaningful.

Go on vacation, just as a family. As kids get older, they want to take friends along everywhere they go. There are times to include friends on excursions and times not to. But most family vacations should be for just the family. When else do you have several days or a week of family time without interruptions? When friends come along, you lose the valuable dimension of one-on-one parent-child communication.

CHAPTER 9

The Fourth "R"

If I asked you to name the "three R's," you probably would automatically rattle off "reading, 'riting, and 'rithmetic." But we need a fourth "R" as we move into the twenty-first century. How about "right from wrong"?

Some kids learn values at home. Their house is their character education classroom because mom and dad have woven character lessons into everyday conversation. They happen spontaneously and regularly, overflowing with values that the parents hold dearly.

But that doesn't happen in most homes. If children don't learn character at home, where do they get it? At school? On TV? Anywhere else?

Character has fallen into a giant sinkhole. Many people are trying to fill it. But with what?

If you're a parent, educator, or church youth leader, you need to be aware of what is going on, what kids are learning as society tries to "educate" them.

Not long ago, the federal government unveiled new public service announcements for television designed to reduce the spread of AIDS. The ads said this: "The message is simple:

when having sex with someone whose sexual history is a sexual mystery, always use a condom."

These ads advance promiscuity and mislead kids to think that condoms will adequately protect them against disease. This is a typical example of "contraception-based" education.

Many people have tried to solve the problem of teen pregnancy with contraceptives and handed them out freely. Yet the teen pregnancy rate has not dropped. Instead, the government budget for contraceptives keeps going up.

Some top elected officials, who consider themselves enlightened, are pushing hard for school health clinics. They want them in every high school in America. These officials are outrageously missing the mark. Giving out contraceptives at school will not reduce teen pregnancies. In fact, I'd like to ask these politicians just which of the following could be eliminated by the use of contraceptives:

Pregnancy? Fear of pregnancy? AIDS? Guilt? Herpes? Parental disappointment? Chlamydia? Syphilis? Embarrassment? Abortion? Shotgun weddings? Gonorrhea? Various other sexually transmitted diseases? Selfishness? Pelvic Inflammatory Disease? Heartbreak? Infertility? Loneliness? Cervical cancer? Poverty? Loss of self-esteem? Loss of reputation? The use of another person for one's own gratification? Suicide? Substance abuse? Melancholy? Loss of faith? Possessiveness? Diminished ability to communicate? Isolation? Loss of friendships? Rebellion against other familiar standards? Alienation? Viewing others as sex objects? Difficulty with long-term commitment? Aggression towards women? Ectopic pregnancy? Sexual violence? Loss of sense of responsibility toward others? Loss of honesty? Jealousy? Depression? Death?

Let me ask again: which of the above could be eliminated by using contraceptives?

High school students hear plenty about contraceptives. But they rarely hear about sexual self-control or choosing a lifestyle of abstinence after becoming sexually active. This secondary virginity is the information they need. The fact that they don't have it saddens me. Most students are not prepared to deal with death and other emotional and physical consequences of their behavior.

"Too many of today's children have straight teeth and crooked morals," stated one high school principal.[1]

Unlike so many so-called "sex experts," when I speak I don't categorize these kids as unfortunate, pathetic, sexually active teens who probably come from single-parent homes, don't use birth control, and would probably continue to be sexually active no matter what anybody said. I see assemblies of young, precious, unique human beings who are capable of self-control, respect, and responsibility in spite of their family situation.

Character when it counts

I agree with Thomas Lickona that one of the "greatest challenges facing our schools today is teaching our children respect, responsibility, hard work, compassion, and other values so desperately needed in today's society. Most parents say they want help from the schools in teaching children a basic sense of right and wrong, but 'values education' can be profoundly controversial, even feared. In a pluralistic society where values often clash, schools struggle with fundamental questions: What values should they teach? And how should they teach them?"[2]

Comprehensive sex education originated in Sweden in the fifties and quickly became the prototype for the Western world. It is based on four premises:

1. Teenage sexual activity is inevitable.
2. Educators should be value-neutral regarding sex.
3. Schools should openly discuss sexual matters.
4. Sex education should teach students about contraception.[3]

What has been the impact of this value-neutral, nondirective information? Teen sexual activity, pregnancies, and abortions all greatly increased!

When AIDS came on the scene, educators added condom instruction and called it "safer sex." They also gave the "Abstinence, but..." message.

This message fails because it tells students to be "responsible" and use contraception. It doesn't give them ethical and moral reasons to wait until marriage. It doesn't help anyone develop self-control nor does it explain the relationship between love and sex.

A civilization is unlikely to survive without such values as self-control, compassion, moderation, generosity, justice, loyalty, honesty, integrity, respect for truth, and respect for others. Children who learn these standards live them out in their communities and relationships. Those who don't develop good character grow up "value-neutral"!

Not too many years ago, parents valued these traits and taught them to their children. They were backed by teaching from community leaders, school personnel, pastors, neighbors, and society in general. So every day the values taught by morally concerned parents were reaffirmed by others.

Today, we don't have that same agreement and common commitment. Too many people have different ideas about where the line should be drawn marking right from wrong. The result is an inconsistent message, particularly about sexual issues.

How do we know if it is wrong? Where should the line be drawn between sexual morality and immorality? A young girl fifteen years old who is defending herself about sleeping with her boyfriend draws the line at "love."

As Josh McDowell puts it in ***Right From Wrong***, "Our children need to be convinced that a standard exists for settling claims about moral knowledge, a standard for right and wrong that exists outside, above, and beyond ourselves."[4]

As Theodore Roosevelt also once said: "to educate a person in mind and not in morals is to educate a menace to society."[5]

Some public schools are doing an excellent job. They provide solid educations, maintain discipline, and emphasize traditional moral values. However, they seem to be in the minority. Too many schools are out of control. They include ideas in the curriculum that undermine ethical behavior and point kids to early sexual and drug experimentation.

Most adults approve of schools giving courses in sex education. However, parents assume these courses are health-oriented and taught within a values framework. They would be shocked to learn their children are being taught how to engage in "safer sex" with no character formation or abstinence. As a parent, you need to find out what is taught at your children's school. Will your kids be exposed to facts they aren't mature enough to handle?

You need to stay politically informed on a local, state, and national level and express your opinion to your representatives. Silence is a vote for more money being spent on contraceptive services and condom distribution in high schools.

There are many places where teens can get condoms. But schools should not be one of them. The school's job is to teach. It must not even appear to approve of something wrong. And it certainly must not give students the equipment to engage in behavior which puts them at risk.

Most schools are straightforward in their message to students about drug use. Teachers highly recommend drug abstinence. A school would undermine its messages if it handed out needles and instructions about reducing the risk of death by drugs. No, schools simply say, "Don't do it. It is harmful behavior." Why can't they be as bold about sex?

Let's face facts. This nation has spent more than $3 billion on sex education programs. Dr. Joe McIlhaney says the "level of sexual activity, the number of teenage pregnancies, and the abortion rate all have gone up almost with direct correlation to the increased amount of money spent on the traditional sex education programs ... [They] seem in some way to be causing young people to increase their sexual activity."[6]

Sex education in public schools has failed.

Marlin Maddoux shared some alarming information in ***What Worries Parents Most:***

> [The failure of sex education] is one of the hidden reasons that abortion/family-planning providers are convincing many high schools to install condom dispensers in restrooms, and to demonstrate them in class. ...Wherever Planned Parenthood has gone in, the pregnancy rate has gone up...
>
> Planned Parenthood's sex education programs and materials are brazenly perverse. They are frequently accentuated with crudely obscene four-letter words and illustrated with ribald nudity. They openly endorse aberrant behavior—homosexuality, masturbation, fornication, incest, and even bestiality—and then they describe that behavior in excruciating detail.
>
> Planned Parenthood is the largest abortion provider in America. Planned Parenthood is a driving force behind the laws that, in most states, allow high school girls to get abortions through the schools without parental consent. Planned Parenthood is also involved in the dispensing of birth control pills and condoms on a scale nothing less than awesome. It is a statistical fact that birth control pills and condoms are generally unreliable in preventing pregnancy, especially when used by children, and usually accompanied by increased sexual activity and rising teen pregnancy rates. This increases the demand for abortion, which is often supplied by Planned Parenthood, the birth-control provider![7]

If none of this works, why do it? Why not try something else? How about character education that emphasizes abstinence?

You may be wondering, is abstinence realistic? The judges

in the Miss Alabama pageant wondered that, too, during my interview. I think my statements surprised them. One asked if young people would listen to me if I talked to them about sexual abstinence.

"Absolutely, they will," I told them, and then I gave them this example.

For many years, Maryland had one of the highest teen pregnancy rates in the country. From 1989 to 1991, the federal government, along with Maryland's governor, promoted an advertising campaign aimed toward children. It emphasized abstinence. And do you know what happened? Teen pregnancy in Maryland decreased 10 percent, the abortion rate decreased 30 percent, and the state saved $46 million dollars in health care costs. Now tell me if that is not realistic!

This successful effort in Maryland happened because influential people—parents, educators, pastors, community leaders—were willing to take a stand. They gave a clear and concise message. "Premarital sex is wrong." There were no mixed messages. These people were willing to shout loud and clear: "Enough is enough! We're through with this garbage!" What happened in Maryland can happen across this nation. But it will take all of us pulling together.

The character crisis evident in our country is like a large snowball rolling downhill. It will keep gaining momentum unless it meets resistance. That's why I believe character education is so important. It provides resistance and the right conditions for a meltdown of that snowball. It paints a line down the center of life's highway.

People, young or old, are likely to cross a line if they don't know it's there. That's why it should be painted with bold brush marks. Make it very visible. The consequences of moving across the line are too devastating. Don't do it. That's what you need to tell the young people you love!

CHAPTER 10

What Motivates Me

People ask, "Amie Beth, why do you do a lot of speaking about healthy sexuality, family values, and character education?"

It's because I care. Today's teenagers are tomorrow's future.

During the last thirty years, violent crime has increased 560 percent in America. Illegitimate births are up more than 400 percent. Divorces have quadrupled, and the number of children living in single-parent homes has tripled. Teen suicide has grown by 200 percent.

Has money solved these problems? Has more education helped? Has increased federal spending been a solution? What about government programs? These have been tried, but they fail to address the core issue. They can't change a person's attitude or values or character.

Newt Gingrich, speaker of the United States House of Representatives, has said a civilization cannot survive with twelve-year-olds having babies, fifteen-year-olds shooting one another, seventeen-year-olds dying of AIDS, and eighteen-year-olds graduating with diplomas they cannot read!

Young people today are hurting. The future of this nation, as we know it, depends on the quality of our youth and the health of the families they will establish one day.

They need facts and *accurate* information. We owe them the truth about health, relationships, marriage, and family values. Teens need to hear over and over again that virginity is a special trust and sexual intimacy a wonderful gift to be discovered within the bounds of marriage. As Max Lucado says in ***A Gentle Thunder***, "Virginity is a rose plucked from the garden, given by God and intended to be shared with your forever partner."[1]

With this book I've tried to provide the facts about sex that are conspicuously absent in the information circulating in the public today. I pray it will motivate you, if you're a teen, to consider the importance of sexual abstinence until you enter into the lifelong commitment of marriage. If one teenager avoids an unplanned pregnancy or a damaging sexually transmitted disease, then the time and energy I put into writing and speaking will not be in vain.

There is another reason why I am sharing this message. It goes much deeper than my concern for teenagers and their families. I believe each individual is unique and special. Every person is precious. This is true, even in the case of the inner-city teenager who stays in and out of trouble, a girl who is seeking her third abortion, or a down-and-outer who is considering suicide. Every single one of us was put on earth for a reason, and we are part of a larger purpose. We are not a product of some cosmic accident. We are unique. We are made in the image of God Himself.

Dear friend, God, our Creator, loves you! He knows you! He cares about you! He calls you by name! That's true no matter who you are or what you've done. He has a plan and a purpose for your life.

Our society has removed the Bible from schools and workplaces. But that doesn't mean its truths are not extremely relevant. People have moved far away from the Ten Commandments, sent by God through Moses. They have reaped disastrous results because they have disobeyed or ignored these commandments. The Bible, God's message to humankind, is the foundation on which I have built my life.

The Bible is God's inspired Word, and the lifestyle it advocates builds a society where human beings can be content and find meaning and happiness. I believe its message with all my heart. It is my manual for life.

The Bible tells where to place the line. It describes the absolutes of good character. People today may try to move the line, obscure it, erase it, or ignore it. That doesn't change the fact that God drew the line to help us know how to live life at His best and please Him, the One who loves us. He doesn't just say in the Bible He loves us; He proves His love.

I once heard a story about a little boy who looked out his window as a terrible storm was raging. He saw a tiny bird flying in circles, trying to escape the storm, before it crashed into his bedroom window. The boy tried hard to show the bird how to find safety in the backyard barn. He ran out and motioned the way. But he couldn't communicate with the small creature or speak its language. Before the storm ended, the bird flew against the window again, breaking its neck.

The next morning, the boy buried it beside the barn. "Oh," he thought, "if I could have become a tiny bird myself, I could have shown the way into the safety of the barn. He would have survived the storm."

That's what God did. He came to us, His creation, through Jesus Christ. For centuries, God sent messengers, but we just couldn't find the safety of the Father's "barn" through them. So God came Himself. He became one of us in flesh and blood to show us the way to safety, to salvation. The first part of the Bible, the Old Testament, predicted Jesus, the Messiah, would come one day. And He did.

I love the Bible verse, "For God so loved the world (that's you and me) that He gave His one and only Son (Jesus), that whoever believes in Him shall not perish but have eternal life (with Jesus forever in His home, heaven)" (John 3:16 NIV).

God cares about each one of us, from the unborn baby to the elderly invalid. Why do I care about the unborn baby? Listen to God's Word about the unborn child:

"For You (God) created my inmost being; You (God) knit me

together in my mother's womb. I praise You because I am fearfully and wonderfully made; Your works are wonderful. . . . My frame was not hidden from You when I was made in the secret place (womb). When I was woven together in the depths of the earth, Your eyes saw my unformed body. All the days ordained for me were written in Your book before one of them came to be" (Psalm 139:13-16 NIV).

God knows and loves the developing baby. He calls the child by name even before its birth. When aborted, the baby, whom God knows and loves and has a life plan for, is killed. The child's future is destroyed. That's the reason why abortion is so terribly wrong. The abortionist is destroying a life God gave to Himself and cherishes. A life God made in His own image.

I came to know God as a young child. I can tell you today Jesus Christ is Lord of my life. He is everything to me. Without Him, I am nothing. All I do, I try to do for Him.

My relationship with Him is what motivates me to talk to teenagers about where they should draw the line personally. Good character flows out of a day-by-day walk with Him. You can have this relationship and the subsequent good character, too, if you are willing to submit to Him.

Solomon summarizes this best by saying, "Fear God and keep His commandments" (Eccl. 12:13 NASB).

God is the ultimate determiner of truth, and He alone defines right and wrong and draws the line for me. By keeping His commandments, through dependence on Him, I can avoid the confusing message our society gives about what truth is and who defines it. Then my decisions are not based on situation ethics, without reference to any standard, but instead are based on His moral absolutes of behavior.

God loves you and me. He created each of us as unique as each snowflake, in His image. We are precious to Him. But God is perfect, and you and I are far from perfect. The whole human race is filled with wrongdoing. Because of this and our personal participation in it, we are separated from God.

But He wanted to do something about this separation. He came to earth in flesh and blood through Jesus, His Son. Jesus died on a cross for you and me. In doing this, He showed us the way to safety, which we call salvation, so we could have a personal relationship with Him, closing the separation forever.

All He asks us to do is to believe and trust that He died in our place. When we do that, God will forgive our sins and give us eternal life. We become His children. Before we were merely His creation. Nothing can ever separate us from Him and His love from that point forward. We acknowledge Him as Lord and build our lives on Him as our foundation. And He prepares a place for us where, one day, we will live forever with Him.

Following Jesus throughout life is not always easy. Christians through the centuries have been called to give their very lives for Him. Others have been laughed at and mocked for believing in Him. But whatever you may go through, when you consider the value of eternal life with God who so dearly loves you, it is worth the price.

Perhaps you're a teenager or adult who has lived what you consider a messed-up life. You would be embarrassed if others knew some of the things you've done. You know your actions were wrong in the sight of a Holy God. The wonderful message that God brought through Jesus is that you can be forgiven for all your wrongdoing: disobedience to your parents, sexual activity outside of marriage, an abortion, whatever. God will forgive you for everything. He loves you and wants you to come to Him, your Creator.

Here is one of the most beautiful stories in the Bible:

Jesus was hanging on the cross, dying for you and me so we might live forever with Him. On each side of Him hung a criminal. These two men had lived hard lives. They were thieves and murderers. Unlike Jesus, they deserved death. One criminal hurled insults at the dying Jesus. "Aren't you the Christ?" he shouted. "Save yourself and us!" That criminal died in the raging storm, alone and eternally forsaken.

But the other, with his dying breath, looked to Jesus and said: "Remember me when you come into your kingdom." He believed and trusted Jesus. In his own way, he asked Jesus into his life to forgive Him for His wrongdoing.

Jesus turned to the believing thief and said, "I tell you the truth, today you will be with me in paradise." That criminal also died, but he did not die alone and was never forsaken. For Jesus had forgiven him and shown him the way into the safety of the barn. The man trusted in Jesus and has eternal life with Him. My prayer for you is that you will believe He will forgive your sins and ask Him to come into your life and give you His peace, power, and eternal life.

You may wish to pray this prayer:

Lord Jesus, thank you for dying on the cross to pay the penalty for my sins. You said in your Word you would come into my life if I asked, so I ask you right now to come in, forgive my sins, give me eternal life, and please be in control of my life. Amen.

If you prayed this prayer, I'd love to hear from you.

CHAPTER 11

My Story

(As told by my mother, Barbara Dickinson)

Tension filled the large concert hall. The young women in their beautiful gowns stood on the massive stage awaiting THE announcement. Within seconds, all would know the identity of Miss Alabama for 1994.

Only the top two awards were left—first runner-up and Miss Alabama. Our daughter, Amie Beth, was a finalist and would soon find out if she would realize her dream. She and Heather Whitestone stood poised among the forty-five contestants. One of the two would become Miss Alabama.

Every muscle in my body tightened as I gazed at Amie Beth. "This next position is very important," the host began. "If, for any reason, the new Miss Alabama cannot fulfill her duties, this young woman will take her place."

To the silent, anticipating crowd, she then loudly announced: "First runner-up is contestant number 19, Miss Samford University, Amie Beth Dickinson!"

My heart sank along with my husband's.

Amie Beth's good friend, Heather Whitestone, was crowned Miss Alabama 1994.

We were excited for Heather, a lovely young woman. She

had overcome profound deafness and successfully competed with the other contestants.

As Amie Beth's family, however, we inwardly groaned with disappointment, and our hearts went out to our daughter. The news had to be painful to her.

Preparing for the pageant had been grueling and exhausting. I compared it to training for the Olympics, involving years of intense discipline and hard work. Every area of competition had to be close to perfect.

Amie Beth had just missed her dream. Or so we thought.

The early years

During those final moments of the pageant, I thought about Amie Beth's discipline and hard work. Together, our family had spent thousands of hours preparing for this event. But my mind also flooded with memories about Amie Beth's past—her birth, adoption, childhood, frustrations, and successes.

For many years, Doug and I tried to have a child. But it didn't happen. We finally decided to adopt and put our name on the public waiting list in Pennsylvania where we lived. For years, we waited in vain for a baby to be placed in our open arms.

As time passed, we worked our way to the top of the list. But no baby came. Soon, due to Doug's medical training, we might have to move. We worried about having to start over at the bottom of a list in another state.

Our situation seemed hopeless.

Doug came home depressed many nights. "Barb," he would say. "Did you know the hospital had more abortions today than deliveries?"

It made no sense. Doug loved children. He would make a great father. I longed for him to have the opportunity.

Finally, we received a call that sent our hopes soaring. A young woman in a reformatory wanted a couple to adopt her baby. We drove through a blizzard to meet her, only to discover she wasn't pregnant.

She had lied, trying to get out of the reformatory. The whole situation made us heartsick. We began to believe we would never become parents.

We had made numerous expensive telephone calls to attorneys and adoption agencies, pursuing every lead. Finally, financially and emotionally drained, Doug and I gave up with broken hearts.

We decided to change direction and planned a short-term move to Africa to work in medical missions. With papers, passports, and immunizations complete, we were ready to leave for a third-world country—or so we thought.

God had other plans for us.

A seventeen-year-old unmarried teenager gave birth to a healthy, dark-haired girl, and the newborn needed a home.

I cannot tell you how excited we were when the chairman of the university's OB/GYN department called. He was Doug's instructor and my physician. A baby, *our* baby, had been born! We quickly unpacked our suitcases, canceled our trip, and made the wonderful adjustment to parenthood.

The celebration

We were living in the tiny servant's quarters of an old farmhouse. It had railroad-car wall sidings, and rent was only $60 a month. Tap water barely flowed through the rusty plumbing. The owner had killed fourteen rats before we moved in.

We attempted to beautify our home. Since we couldn't afford to buy anything, we spent weekends digging shrubs out of the woods and planting them in our bare front yard. The room chosen for our nursery was the size of some of today's closets—a little more than nine feet square. It had shocking pink walls and ceilings. We applied four coats of white paint to cover the screaming color!

Amie Beth's pediatrician brought her to our tiny home. As soon as he placed her in my arms, I was struck by her beauty.

She had dark eyebrows and bright blue eyes. I'll never forget the look on Doug's face when he saw his daughter. It was love at first sight.

We welcomed her with a huge celebration. Relatives traveled from distant states to rejoice with us. She was the center of attention. We watched every move, every sound of this beautiful baby. Doug and I eagerly took turns cuddling, feeding, and rocking her.

After four joyful months of parenthood, Doug moved to Alabama to start his internship. Amie Beth and I, with our collie, Duffie, followed later. Three months alone in Alabama were difficult for Doug. He missed us but stayed very busy training in his medical specialty.

When our baby turned two weeks old, we began a special bedtime routine. As we tucked her in, we told her about how she came to be ours. We would end the story each night, "Amie Beth, God loves you and has a wonderful plan for your life, and He chose us to be your mom and dad and for you to be part of our family." We always reminded her how precious she was and how we had prayed for her for years. By school age, Amie Beth understood adoption is a very special process. She accepted this because she was so loved and wanted and was our gift from God.

Amie Beth was intelligent and did well academically, but she struggled with math. For years, even after Doug had worked fourteen to sixteen hours a day, he would come home, kiss me hello, and walk straight to Amie Beth's room. Some of my favorite memories are the times I saw Doug on the floor, tutoring her in math. There he would sit, in his white coat with his stethoscope still hanging around his neck, patiently helping her prepare for a math test.

Over the next few years, Doug and I were blessed with two more children: a son, Chip, and a daughter, Arden. Both came to us through private adoption. Doug repeated his math lessons over and over with both Chip and Arden. We always mused this was God's way of bonding Doug and his children.

Self-esteem building

When Amie Beth was very young, a neighbor suggested I read ***Hide and Seek*** by James Dobson. The book was required reading where she taught school. I couldn't put it down. Dobson's concepts helped me immensely in rearing Amie Beth, Chip, and Arden.

Dobson says developing a natural talent is important in building a child's self-esteem. Taking this advice, we experimented to find Amie Beth's talents. It turned out she had many.

She loved to read. In the first grade, she read ninety-nine books, one less than the winner of the contest.

Ballet came quite naturally to her, and she worked hard at it. In the eighth grade, a teacher suggested we send Amie Beth to ballet school in New York. "She has the perfect ballet body," she told us. We decided to keep her at home. It was the right decision.

In the third grade, Amie Beth began piano lessons. She practiced and did well. Years later, she won several talent awards for her music.

She was quite naturally a communicator and actress. At age five, she grabbed my tape recorder one evening and stretched out on our bed. We listened from behind the door as she imitated the television news commentators.

In the sixth grade, Amie Beth asked if she could audition for Summerfest in Birmingham. This was a high-caliber theater production using Hollywood actors and actresses combined with local talent. We didn't realize our daughter could sing! But she amazed us with a beautiful voice as she practiced. After two weeks of intense dancing, acting, and singing in the Summerfest workshop, Amie Beth was chosen from 250 girls as one of the eight orphans in ***Annie***. And she was selected for a solo singing part.

This acting opportunity was pivotal. From then on, the stage became a major part of her life.

By seventh grade, she decided to try out for ***Kids' World***, a Saturday morning news show on our local NBC affiliate. For the next several years, she anchored it every three or four weeks.

She was a cheerleader in junior and senior high. At Briarwood Christian High School, she was Maria in the school play, ***West Side Story***, and was elected the first female president at Briarwood. For three years, Amie Beth served as a class officer and student government leader.

Pageants and platforms

We never encouraged her to compete in pageants, but she became interested on her own in the Miss Alabama Scholarship Pageant. Eventually winning the Miss Alabama title became her dream.

"When Amie Beth shared the idea about entering a pageant, I was very much opposed to it," Doug remembers. "I had no idea what this program was about. Like many men and women, I thought it was simply a 'beauty' contest."

As time passed, Doug realized the Miss America process emphasized the whole person—physical fitness, communication, poise, grace, talent development, and community service. The bulk of the scoring, however, centered on talent and interview skills.

In 1991, her senior year, she entered the Shelby County Junior Miss pageant, a sister pageant to the Miss Alabama scholarship program. She was second runner-up. After graduation, she competed for the Miss Shelby County title, a Miss Alabama preliminary, and was named first runner-up.

The next year, she entered the Miss Shelby County pageant again. This time, Amie Beth wanted to choose a platform that came from her heart. Through their platforms, contestants were required to take stands on issues they believed were relevant to society. Many chose topics like "teens against drunk driving," "child abuse," or other non-controversial issues.

Amie Beth, her college roommate, Doug, and I, had a brainstorming session for a platform topic. Her roommate asked, "Why don't you choose sexual abstinence? That would be great since you are adopted and it's so important to you."

We liked the idea, although it would be controversial and at that time "politically incorrect." The "safer sex" concept was being widely promoted through school health clinics. Amie Beth disagreed with this approach and carefully researched abstinence education in order to write the pageant's required platform paper.

This time, she won! Becoming Miss Shelby County opened doors in the public schools to promote the Miss Alabama scholarship program. Amie Beth soon discovered, though, the girls were also interested in hearing her talk about sexual abstinence.

She rapidly became well known for her encouraging abstinence talks. Churches and Christian schools began to contact her to speak to their students. Because many educators regarded sexual abstinence to be a religious issue, church invitations far outnumbered those from private and public schools. It didn't take long for her to earn the respect of people who worked with young people from all walks of life. But teens everywhere needed to hear the message. Amie Beth wanted to expand her audience to include public-school students as well.

In June 1992, Amie Beth competed for Miss Alabama.

Amie Beth did not place in the top ten that first year at the state level. In fact, she didn't believe she did well at all. At the interview, the judges asked tough questions, including some about surrogate motherhood and artificial insemination, in addition to those about her platform, sexual abstinence.

"Just how realistic is this abstinence platform?" a judge inquired in a condescending voice. She knew most contestants were tested in some way, that it was part of it, and she needed to be tough. But she felt belittled and broke down and cried as she left.

Amie Beth said after the pageant, "I feel compelled to speak to middle schools and high schools about saying no to peer pressure. I want them to understand the errors they are hearing in public-school sex education about `safe' sex. I've seen their faces. I've heard their hurting hearts. They know I have the answer and that I believe in them."

Competing again for Miss Alabama would have opened doors, but she wasn't sure she wanted to repeat the exhausting preparation.

She wanted, however, to continue speaking to kids about unhealthy sexual behavior. We called a friend, Wales Goebel, who had a high-school ministry. He suggested Amie Beth contact the local Sav-a-Life organization, which he founded. He mentioned a program they sponsored called SAFE (Sex and Family Education) and asked her to talk with Ruth Wooten, the director.

This was a big step because SAFE was welcome in many public schools and churches. They trained Amie Beth to be a presenter, and she frequently spoke on behalf of SAFE. The team for these three-day seminars also included a physician and/or nurse who shared the medical aspects of sexually transmitted diseases. However, Amie Beth's individual demand as a speaker was increasing as well.

A wonderful opportunity opened through a good friend, Aimee Barrett, a student at Auburn University. Aimee's professor had invited people representing different lifestyles to speak to the class. She included gays, lesbians, and single-parents, but no one who spoke on behalf of sexual abstinence. Aimee asked her professor to consider inviting someone to address the abstinence viewpoint and recommended Amie Beth. The professor called me to check on Amie Beth's qualifications and background to address this college audience.

The professor agreed to let her speak along with her Dad, who is a physician. Doug spoke on the medical aspects of sexually transmitted diseases. Amie Beth talked about the emotional and physical consequences of premature sexual activity. She stated responsible sexual behavior needs to be based on fidelity, commitment, and maturity—placing sexual activity within the context of marriage.

Doug said you could hear a pin drop. The students responded favorably. I thought, "How gutsy."

This proved a major turning point in Amie Beth's life.

Speaking requests increased.

She soon was invited to speak to the Sylacauga County School Board on behalf of putting abstinence education into the curriculum. There she met a very important woman who sharpened her mission. Maureen Duran was a fireball! She and Amie Beth "clicked" immediately. This was the beginning of a long and close relationship for both Amie Beth and me.

Maureen is the mother of five small children and lives in Virginia. She was dedicated to and enthusiastic about building character in kids. She served as education director of Teen Choice, a pilot program for abstinence under the Bush administration. Maureen gave good advice on writing and speaking and opened up a new world of opportunity. She continues to help Amie Beth with speeches and supplies her with relevant information.

The state AIDS symposium invited Amie Beth to address a large group of health-care professionals. She and Maureen worked together on the speech. Amie Beth prepared for a solid six months. She was able to introduce the concept of character-based sexuality to many conference attendees. Few people realized that children cannot be taught about sex education principles until they possess character traits such as self-control, honesty, respect, kindness, compassion, etc. Character traits are essential in practicing refusal and cessation skills. The enthusiastic response to her speech thrilled us all.

Wherever she spoke, school officials and teachers were amazed at how Amie Beth held the attention of the overwhelming majority of kids. She was warmly received and related well to kids. Her speaking invitations became overwhelming. I spent five to six hours each day coordinating her schedule.

She next won the Miss East Alabama pageant. During this Miss Alabama preliminary, she met Steven Ball, one of the Miss East Alabama judges. He later became very important in her preparations.

In the 1993 statewide Miss Alabama competition, she placed fourth runner-up. The five judges came from different parts of the United States and held a wide range of political and ethical positions. This year she also won the prestigious Nora Chapman Interview Award. I realized then it was possible for our daughter to become Miss Alabama someday with her platform.

She decided to give it one more try. In November, Amie Beth won the Miss Samford University preliminary. Representing her school meant the world to her.

In June 1994, Amie Beth tried a final time for the Miss Alabama crown. She kept her sexual abstinence platform, which she now called character education.

When you get to the "top five," abilities are somewhat equal. The winner is usually the one who fine-tunes the most in the closing months. We had our work cut out for us.

We made numerous trips to Atlanta where Steven Ball taught Amie Beth how to present herself on stage in all areas of competition. He emphasized the importance of confidence and gave her the encouragement she needed.

Maureen Duran provided needed information and tips for the all-important Miss Alabama interview. Other valuable assistance came from the Reverend Mark Roessler of Briarwood Presbyterian Church. He taught her how to debate controversial topics without compromising her beliefs. She learned to express opinions which differed sharply from the beliefs of some judges. He helped her display authority in her answers without an "in-your-face" approach.

Eleanor Trafton, Amie Beth's piano teacher, confidant, arranger, and inspiration, prepared her for the talent competition. They decided she would play "Chopsticks", Liberace-style. This popular piece was a very difficult arrangement technically. It highlighted her musical gift and brought out her performing personality. Eleanor's help was crucial because those who received high talent scores were usually college music majors. But Amie Beth was not.

After nine months of lessons and daily practice, Amie Beth perfected "Chopsticks" and was eager to perform. She practiced so long and hard that she had calluses on her fingertips.

Doug and I spent hours cutting out newspaper editorials

from the **Wall Street Journal** and **USA Today**. He discussed important events and newsworthy issues with Amie Beth, and we held family "interviews." Doug had a soft way of discussing controversial topics and demonstrated this for her. She filed relevant articles in a large notebook. She studied the material daily and listened to international news on National Public Radio. She had no idea what the judges would ask and wanted to be well prepared.

We set up mock interviews with people from different walks of life. They asked difficult questions, which she taped along with her responses. She then discovered where she was strong or needed more work.

Amie Beth continued to speak on abstinence and character, but there were those who discouraged her. They said abstinence was too controversial and not politically correct. They said she probably couldn't win with that platform. But God directed her differently, and Amie Beth refused to change her platform.

Doug and I watched Amie Beth become very disciplined. She had maintained a daily time alone with God since before the seventh grade. As a teenager, she began writing in a journal during her quiet time. This was her way of communicating with God as she prayed.

She rarely missed an exercise workout. These physical and spiritual disciplines boosted her self-confidence more than anything.

The pageant emphasizes the importance of excellent grades, so Amie Beth tried hard to excel academically in the midst of all of the other time-consuming activities going on in her life.

The pageant was a sacrifice for all of us—Doug and me, Chip, and Arden. It was difficult coordinating the family unit at times, but everyone worked together to support each other.

The competition

Amie Beth knew her strongest competition: Heather Whitestone and Leigh Sherer. Heather had been first runner-up for Miss Alabama two years in a row. Leigh was a beautiful, graceful vocal and piano performance major in college. This was the third year of competition for each of them.

You could feel the excitement as pageant week approached. On Monday morning, forty-five excited, beautiful young women checked into Samford University. The public preliminaries took three nights. On Wednesday evening, Amie Beth competed in the evening gown category. She was judged on grace, poise, and speaking ability. She gave a twenty-second statement on stage about her platform. On Thursday night, she performed her "Chopsticks" piano arrangement. And on Friday night, she competed in swimsuit.

Heather, Leigh, and Amie Beth all won talent preliminaries in their respective groups. Amie Beth also took honors in swimsuit competition. On Saturday, she was given again, for the second year, the Nora Chapman Interview Award as well as the Virginia McDormitt Community Service Award.

The judges were truly interested and surprised by Amie Beth's widespread appeal as she shared her commitment to sexual purity and character education. Her reputation spilled over into other states.

Going into the top-ten finals Saturday night, Amie Beth and Heather were the only double preliminary winners. The two were going down to the wire. Everyone seemed convinced Miss Alabama would either be Amie Beth or Heather.

During the interview, Amie Beth was asked, "You are competing against a profoundly deaf individual. What do you think about that?"

She smiled warmly, made eye contact with the judges, and responded with confidence: "I think we all have areas of weakness or some disability. Somewhere within us we have something we have to overcome. I would only ask that you be fair."

After Heather won, Amie Beth and I made plans to go to

Atlantic City to support her as she competed for Miss America in September. Journalist Adam Colwell described those final moments of the national pageant:

"All eyes were turned toward the two contestants standing alone at the front of the great stage. Millions of others watched on television, awaiting the words that would reveal the identity of the nation's new beauty queen. As Miss Alabama, Heather Whitestone, was crowned as the new Miss America amidst hugs and tears, another beauty from the Yellowhammer State was exulting as she and her mom sat in the audience.

"Twenty-two-year-old Amie Beth Dickinson had finished second to Heather in the Miss Alabama pageant, falling just short of her dream of representing her state....

Her life was about to dramatically change."

On September 17, she woke up as Amie Beth Dickinson. She went to bed that night as Miss Alabama. She had realized her dream.

***

As parents, we are indebted to and remain thankful for the Miss Alabama organization and their voluntary, encouraging, and sacrificial service to our daughter. Through their selfless efforts, Amie Beth reached a new plateau of personal achievement. She was able to become a blessing to so many around the state.

Being Miss Alabama is like having a job—with many benefits and responsibilities. Benefits came her way through an overwhelming number of opportunities made possible through sponsors and hundreds of volunteers. There is only one paid employee of the Miss Alabama organization, its secretary. That is awesome.

Amie Beth had a responsibility to represent her state and abide by the Miss Alabama rules—which she did gladly. For every rule, there was a reason. We came to appreciate this organization's efforts in structuring such a well-organized and meaningful program. After all, their reputation preceded them in producing major candidates for the Miss America title.

Sponsors supplied a car, gas, clothing, hair and nail needs, dry-cleaning services, photography and video expertise, a watch, camera, scholarship money, and so much more. It would be difficult to name them all.

Traveling companions never left her side and were available for encouragement, direction, and simple friendship. They laughed and cried together. She drew close to them all and loved and appreciated each and every one. It was so apparent that they believed in providing for Miss Alabama every opportunity for success in personal achievement.

Doug and I cannot thank each one by name, but they know who they are, and we will forever be in their debt.

Numerous opportunities to speak about character education, emphasizing sexual abstinence, were a wonderful benefit from the Miss Alabama title. She has addressed tens of thousands of educators, parents, pastors, and teenagers. After crowning Leigh Sherer as the new Miss Alabama in 1995, she has continued to receive speaking invitations. Her message is very important to her. And it's one we all need to hear. Her mission is:

• Challenging teens to take responsibility for this generation and the next through character-based education.

• Assisting others in understanding that character education is based on the belief that drug abuse, alcohol abuse, and sexual promiscuity all share a common core—the absence of good character.

• Impressing upon parents, teachers, youth workers, pastors, neighbors, and most of all, teens, that sexual abstinence can be maintained until marriage.

• Helping teens avoid unplanned pregnancies and damaging sexually transmitted disease.

• Teaching teens the truth about health, relationships, marriage, and family values.

I believe God is only beginning to fulfill those words we whispered over Amie Beth's crib each night: "God has a wonderful plan for your life...."

nie Beth at six months.

Amie Beth was certainly the "apple" of her Daddy's eye.

completed family—Arden, two and a half years;
o, ten years; and Amie Beth, twelve.

Amie Beth loved performing, even at weddings (with cousin Jeff).

date (Valentine banquet with Jeff Kim).

Dear friend Kim Till with Amie Beth, both varsity cheerleaders.

▲ *Doug and I were blessed with three precious children, Amie Beth, Arden, and Chip.*

▼ *The kids maternal side of the family. Nana and Grampa Wills stressed the importance of being together as a family no matter what it took.*

Our three kids and Mattie, our cat.

I was given a wonderful husband.

Amie Beth as Miss Shelby County 1992.

Amie Beth performs ballet as Miss Alabama at the 1995 Miss Alabama pageant.

▲ *"Oh, Ashley, Ashley—tell me you love me Ashley." A comedy piano rendition of "Tara's Theme" brought the house down with laughter as she performed at the 1995 Miss Alabama pageant.*

▲ *Chosen as the master of ceremonies for 1996 Miss Alabama Pageant. Picture backstage with friend and contestant Julianne Anderson and Betty Ponder (designer of the dresses Amie Beth wor that week). This silver one was my favorite!*

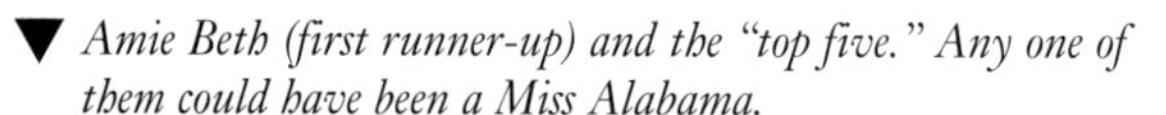

▼ *Amie Beth (first runner-up) and the "top five." Any one of them could have been a Miss Alabama.*

Amie Beth crowned by Heather as Miss Alabama 1994.

What an honor for Amie Beth to share the podium with Dan Quayle.

Amie Beth being interviewed for TV before the Eighth Annual State AIDS Symposium.

Last minute instructions from our Miss Alabama Board president, Nan Teninbaum.

Top to bottom left to right
1. Amie Beth speaking at McGill-Toolen High School in Mobile, Alabama.
2. Amie Beth's favorite illustration using a tennis racquet.
3. Miss Alabama 1994. She loved to speak to kids!
4. Kids gather round for autographs.
5. Amie Beth related well to teens.
6. Talking before the Eighth Annual State AIDS Symposium.

Amie Beth's sincerity was always obvious as she spoke.

Appendix A

100 Ways to Promote Character Education

Recommendations from the Center for the Advancement of Ethics and Character, Boston University

1. Hang pictures of heroes and heroines in halls and classrooms.
2. Institute a student-tutoring program.
3. Promote service clubs with real missions for the school community.
4. Be vigilant about preventing and stopping scapegoating of one child by other children.
5. Create recognition programs that acknowledge some thing besides academic, athletic, or artistic achievement.
6. Seriously and thoughtfully grade student behavior and contribution to the community.
7. Create a code of behavior for your classroom (and school) to which students and teacher agree.
8. Invite parents to observe and contribute to your class room.

9. Choose a personal motto and share it with your students.
10. Promote a "virtue of the month" and study it.
11. Share a personal hero and tell the students why he or she is your hero.
12. Regularly weave into your teaching of stories, history, and other subjects the question, "What's the right thing to do?" Follow up with a discussion.
13. Help students see that the "good" in students is more than academic success.
14. Treat ethical issues like other intellectual issues—get the facts, gather evidence,weigh consequences, and make a decision.
15. Structure opportunities for your students to do service in the community.
16. Lead by example. For instance, pick up the discarded piece of paper in the hall. Clean the chalkboard out of respect for the next teacher.
17. Don't allow unkindness of any kind in your classrooms.
18. Don't permit swearing or vulgar or obscene language in the classroom or anywhere on school property.
19. Involve parents in student misbehavior through notes, calls, visits.
20. Write, call, or visit parents to praise their child.
21. Make it clear that students have a moral responsibility to work hard in school.
22. Use ethical language with faculty colleagues. "I have a responsibility to...," "The courage of her convictions caused her to...," "My neglect led him to...."
23. Include the study of "local heroes" in your social studies classes.
24. Institute an honor system for test-taking and homework assignments.
25. Create a charity. Collect donations, and urge students to decide on their distribution.
26. Reinforce the moral authority of parents, urging students to take their moral problems to their parents.

Discuss with students why this is sometimes difficult.

27. Post on the wall sayings that encourage good character, such as, "Don't wait to be a great person; start now!"
28. Share stories of ethical conflict, especially those involving students in their present setting. Don't hesitate to write stories and let students struggle to put their views on paper.
29. Celebrate birthdays of heroes and heroines with observance and/or discussion of their accomplishments.
30. Ask students to write their own significant sayings, and display these on walls.
31. Reward students for bringing in articles about ethical and moral issues. Use them in class discussion.
32. Discuss campus "issues of character" on a regular basis (vandalism, good deeds, etc.).
33. Make classroom expectations clear, and hold students accountable for them.
34. Strive to be consistent in dealing with students; avoid allowing personal feelings to interfere with fairness.
35. Admit mistakes, and seek to correct them. Expect and encourage students to do the same.
36. Read aloud a "two-minute story" every day to begin and end the school day. Choose stories that are brief yet value-centered.
37. Consider ethical implications when establishing class room and school policies and procedures; be aware of what messages they send to students.
38. Explain the reason for a particular school or classroom policy, action, or decision. Help students to understand "why," not just "what."
39. Lead students to discuss the ethical and character-developing elements of being a good student.
40. Teach students about competition, helping them see when it is valuable and when it is not.
41. Talk to students about why you are a teacher. Explain how you understand the responsibility and importance

of teaching.

42. Let your students know about your community service. Tell them about volunteering in a food bank, coaching Little League, or teaching at your place of worship.
43. Teach students to analyze the media critically. To what extent do their messages encourage living a life of character?
44. Bring recent high-school graduates to talk about their successful transitions to college, work, or the military. Ask them how good moral habits have helped in their adjustments.
45. Invite local adults to talk about how they have integrated the concept of character into their adult lives.
46. Help reinforce students' empathy. Ask them questions like, "How would you feel if no one would play with you?" or "How would you feel if someone made fun of your name because they thought it was strange sounding?"
47. When conflicts arise at school, teach students the importance of respect, open-mindedness, privacy, and discretion. Do not allow conversations that are fueled by gossip or disrespect.
48. Overtly teach courtesy. Teach students how to listen attentively to other students and adults and avoid interrupting people.
49. Read and discuss biographies of accomplished individuals. Encourage students in upper grades to be discerning, seeing that an individual may have flaws but still be capable of much admirable action.
50. Assign older students to assist younger ones, such as seniors paired with freshmen to show them the school.
51. Emphasize from the first day of class the importance of working hard and striving for certain standards of achievement.
52. Encourage high-school students to become more active in their community by attending city, town, or school board meetings.

53. During the election season, encourage students to research the candidates' positions.
54. Encourage high-school students to volunteer for voter registration drives and, if eligible, to vote.
55. Teach students how to write thank-you notes. As a class, write thank-you notes to people who have done thoughtful things for the students.
56. Give students sufficient feedback when evaluating their work. Demonstrate to students that you are making an effort to communicate to them how they are succeeding and how they can improve.
57. Lead older students to sponsor a pot-luck supper for their parents. Encourage them to cook, decorate, serve and clean up.
58. Begin a monthly "gift-giving" from your class. Suggest that the class perform a service to the school, such as decorating a hallway.
59. Work together as a class or school to clean classrooms or school grounds on a regular basis.
60. Demonstrate your respect for other religions and cultures. Talk to students about the moral imperative to act justly toward others.
61. Stand up for the "underdog," when he or she is being treated unfairly. Use this as a teaching moment.
62. Encourage children in self-contained classrooms to take turns caring for their class pets, taking them home on weekends or holidays. Talk to them about the need to care for other living creatures.
63. Start or expand a class or school recycling program. Talk about the general principles of carefully using what you have and not wasting.
64. Highlight certain programs in your school that may already be emphasizing character, such as S.A.D.D. or the National Honor Society.
65. Suggest that student volunteers clean up the community. With parental support, encourage them to build a community playground, pick up litter, rake

leaves, grow plants, paint a mural on the side of the building, or clean up a local beach.

66. Dust off the school song (alma mater). Teach students, especially the newest ones, the words; talk about their meaning; and include it at every school activity.
67. If your school doesn't have a school song, sponsor some sort of contest for students to write one. As a school community, talk about what kinds of ideas should be included in the school song.
68. Emphasize and teach the significance of school rituals. Talk about the importance of recognizing certain rites as a community and properly acknowledging them.
69. Encourage students to look in on elderly or sick neighbors, particularly during harsh winter months.
70. Start a pen pal exchange between your students and students from a distant state or country. Share the information your students learn about their pen pals' lives. Encourage discussions about what life must be like living in that community.
71. Use the curriculum to teach character. For example, in language arts class, ask students to assume a character's point of view and write about it. Regularly ask questions requiring students to "walk in someone else's shoes."
72. Use constructive criticism tempered by compassion. Help students do the same with each other.
73. Emphasize good sportsmanship in sports, games, and daily interaction with others.
74. When making school policy, allow students' participation and responsibility in some decisions. Urge them to research the ramifications of different policies and present their findings to the administrators and faculty for discussion.
75. Collect interesting, thought-provoking quotes worthy of reflections, discussion, and writing. Here is one example: "The truth never becomes clear as long as we assume that each one of us, individually, is the center of

the universe" (Thomas Merton). Ask students to do the same.

76. Develop a list of suggested readings in character education that teachers and administrators can use as resources.
77. Develop a school motto.
78. Institute a character honor roll.
79. Foster the development of students' self-esteem by providing opportunities for genuine academic and social challenge and achievement.
80. Include in faculty/staff meetings and workshops discussions of the school's "moral climate" and the desired goals for the moral life of the school.
81. Develop a "school code of ethics." Refer to it in all school activities and policy. Disseminate it to all school members. Display it prominently throughout the building.
82. Begin an "exchange network" or "bulletin board" by which teachers and administrators can share their own "100 Ways to Promote Character Education."
83. Include anecdotes of commendable student behavior in the school newsletter to parents.
84. Start a school scrapbook with photos, news stories, and memorabilia reflecting the school's history and accomplishments. Include all school members in contributing to and maintaining the collection. Show it off to school visitors.
85. Publicly recognize the work and achievements of the school's "unsung heroes"—the custodians, repairmen, secretaries, cafeteria workers, and volunteers—who keep things running every day.
86. Assign reasonable amounts of homework that stimulate and challenge students while teaching the importance of self-discipline and perseverance in learning.
87. Design a school pledge that students recite weekly. Include it in school documents, especially those intended for parents.

88. Institute a dress code, explaining its role in promoting an educational environment conducive to learning.
89. Use homeroom periods for activities that develop community and cohesion among students, and a sense of attachment to their school.
90. Create opportunities for parents and students to work together on a school project—for example, a dance, symposium, dinner, or field trip.
91. Be attentive to the physical appearance of the building. Involve all school members in the shared responsibility of general cleanliness and order.
92. Seek ways to involve local business in the life of the school, perhaps through mentoring opportunities or partnerships with student groups.
93. Establish a newcomers' club for newly hired personnel and entering students.
94. Invite local employers to talk to students about the importance of good moral character in the world of work.
95. Urge athletes and coaches to collaborate to develop a code of ethics for athletics.
96. Sponsor a public forum on character education in your community.
97. Ask each organization to design a logo symbolizing a character trait representative of the club's mission.
98. Provide a bimonthly occasion for teachers to gather with their colleagues and study a selection of literature, history, philosophy, or other subject area that relates to ethics.
99. Develop for parents a bibliography of books they can read with their children to stimulate conversation about good character.
100. Sponsor an after-school reading club for students, with age-appropriate literature focused on ending with moral lessons.

Appendix B

Character and Sex Education Resource Guide

Perhaps you're a parent who wishes to know more about issues that affect your teen. Or, you're a teacher concerned about the character education of students. You may be a pastor or youth minister who wants students in your group to learn to resist sexual temptations. Through your efforts, teens can learn how to have an abstinence-based lifestyle until marriage. You will first need good materials. Listed below are resources to assist you in teaching character development. This is by no means a comprehensive list, but it is a place to start.

Curriculum guide

Best Friends
2000 North St., NW, Suite 201
Washington, DC 20036
Phone: (202) 822-9266

Best Friends is an excellent mentoring program for girls in middle school through high school. The program's success depends on the commitment level of the school guidance counselors or mentors themselves. It focuses on abstinence and other issues such as self-esteem, relationships, career goals and peer pressure.

Center for the 4th and 5th R's
State University College at Cortland
P.O. Box 2000
Cortland, NY 13045
Phone: (607) 735-2455, 753-2705.

Thomas Lickona is a nationally known speaker and author on character education and the importance of character in sexuality education. A behavioral psychologist and author of ***Educating for Character***, he is professor of education at State University of New York at Cortland.

The Council for Religion in Independent Schools
P.O. Box 40613
Washington, DC 20016
Phone: (301) 657-0912

"Values In Action: A Middle School Ethics Course" features detailed lesson plans. It uses plays, novels, and films that depict men and women with admirable character traits to inspire students to form values they are willing to act on.

Curriculum guide

Creating Positive Relationships (CPR)
30 N. Rangeline Road, Suite A
Carmel, IN 46032
Phone: (317) 846-0386

Building Healthy Relationships, a not-for-profit organization, offers a curriculum for middle school. It teaches that abstinence from sexual activity before marriage is the best standard of behavior and benefits the physical, mental, social, and emotional well-being of the student. It does not promote birth-control methods.

Educational Guidance Institute
188 Berbusse Lane
Front Royal, VA 22630
Phone: (540) 635-4420

This organization is a resource for parents and schools needing information on healthy sexuality education. The manual ***Foundations for Family Life Education*** provides clear guidelines for family-centered sexuality education. It also offers ***Love and Marriage at the Movies: Educating for Character Through the Film Classics***.

Ethics Resource Center
1120 "G" Street, NW, Suite 200
Washington, DC 20005
Phone: (202) 434-8478

Ethics Resource Center produces videos to help teachers develop and reinforce positive values and character traits in students. ***What Should You Do? Deciding What's Right*** is aimed at grades 4-6. ***Not for Sale. Ethics for the American Workplace*** offers high-school students an introduction to the relationship between personal morality, professional responsibility, and business ethics.

Curriculum guide

Heartwood Institute
425 N. Craig, Suite 302
Pittsburgh, PA 15213
Phone: (412) 688-8570

Friends First clubs provide peer mentoring as well as a speaker/resource network. Why Am I Tempted? (WAIT training) targets public high school students and addresses the issue of abstinence in a classroom or assembly setting. STARS (Students Teaching and Respecting Sexuality) is appropriate for middle schools.

Jeremiah Films
Dept. B
P.O. Box 1710
Hemet, CA 92343
Phone: (800) 828-2290

In "No Second Chance," Cathy Kay, a registered nurse, discusses issues surrounding AIDS and methods of avoiding this life-threatening disease. Self-control is discussed as an essential character trait that all young people need when making sexual decisions. This film is for middle school and up.

The Loving Well Project
Nancy McLaren, coordinator
Boston University School of Education
605 Commonwealth Avenue
Boston, MA 02215
Phone: (617) 353-4088

"The Art of Loving Well" was developed by the College of Communication and the School of Education at Boston University and emphasizes relationship education. It teaches the values of committed, faithful love and friendship through literature. It uses fairy tales, poetry, classic short stories, and

Curriculum guide

contemporary pieces, ranging from "Beauty and the Beast," Greek fables, and Brothers Grimm to Shakespeare, Tolstoy, and John Updike. It was field-tested by 10,000 eighth and ninth-grade students in several states under a five-year grant from U.S. Department of Health and Human Services. Although it is used most often in English or health education classes, it is also appropriate for grades 7-12 in a variety of classroom settings. This curriculum is now distributed nationally.

Project Reality
P.O. Box 97
Golf, IL 60029
Phone: (847) 729-3298
"Choosing the Best" is a values-based, abstinence-focused curriculum for seventh through ninth graders. Through a variety of videos, real-life case studies, role plays, and small group discussions, students benefit from a "self-discovery" learning environment. "Facing Reality" is a similar curriculum that targets students in grades ten through twelve. Both include an AIDS awareness section.

RSVP
6617 Shenandoah
Reynoldsburg, OH 43068
Phone: (614) 864-7787 or (216) 996-4220
"Responsible Social Values Program" (RSVP) offers curriculum for two age groupings. Students in grades K-5 receive character education through multi-cultural literature and activities such as theater, music, dance, and art. Students in grades 6-8 learn about abstinence from sex and illegal substance abuse by using games, "science-magic" tricks, and role plays. Training is available.
Resource: RSVP offers on-campus presentations about drugs, abstinence, and character education. Drama troops perform across the nation, and scripts are available for groups interested in staging their own performances

Curriculum guide

STARS
P.O. Box 8936
Chattanooga, TN 37411
Phone: (800) 477-8277

"Secret Adventures" features Drea Thomas, a seventh-grader with a knack for baby-sitting and the most fantastic bag of tricks since Mary Poppins. In each episode, she takes Matt and Rebecca Long on an animated adventure that teaches all three helpful and important character traits (honesty, responsibility, cooperation, and respect) and conflict resolution skills.

"Everyone Is Not Doing It" is a series of four videos, each 45-minutes long, to help students cope with pressures regarding sex. Topics include behaviors and consequences, how to say no, self-respect, self-control, health risks, and effective love. This series is used in over 3,000 schools.

Resource: "Classroom of the Heart" features Guy Doud, a National Teacher of the Year. It uses humor and warmth to help young people discover their own worth by recognizing worth in others. Guy's talk in a high-school classroom is powerfully intertwined with the dramatized true account of a student with cancer.

Resource: "But Is It Safe?" features Miles McPherson who talks to young people about sexually transmitted diseases, AIDS, abstinence, and condom education. This two-part video takes students through a lively, open, and honest question-and-answer session. Each part is 20-minutes long.

Teen Aid
E. 723 Jackson
Spokane, WA 99207
Phone: (509) 482-2868

"HIV, You Can Live Without It," for grades 5-12, emphasizes abstinence from premarital sexual activity as the best and only sure prevention of AIDS and other sexually transmitted diseases. AIDS is treated in an age-appropriate manner for each grade level.

"Me, My World, My Future" is designed for middle school students. It

Curriculum guide

stresses postponing immediate gratification related to sexual activity, drugs, alcohol, and tobacco and contains convenient and inexpensive "Parent-grams" to promote parent-teen communication. In its third edition, it is based on five years of federally-sponsored research.

Resource: If You Love Me...Show Me," a fully animated video, tells the story of two teenagers and their struggle with sexuality. How do they know they're in love? How about sex? Yes? No? How far is too far? Funny and fast-paced, this story shows the importance of courage and convictions.

Resource: In "Peer Pressure: When the Heat's On," teens reveal real-life pressures and explain how they cope. This film features dramatizations by young actors and discussions with Christopher Ewing, a professional actor. It also includes a student workbook.

Resource: "Who Do You Listen To? Choosing Sexual Abstinence" is a film for adolescents.

Teen Choice
Maureen Duran
15100 General Stevens Court
Chantilly, VA 22021-1320
Phone: (703) 263-1102

"Reasonable Reasons to Wait" is a character-based sexuality education curriculum for middle school and high school students. It teaches teenagers how to practice sexual self-control and helps them develop positive attitudes about sexuality. The first three units are age-appropriate for middle schools. Topics include human sexuality, refusal and cessation skills, dating, and relationships. Students learn such values as making good decisions, respect for others, self-control, and courage. The program includes a two-week peer mentoring program for students in the upper grades and uses separate manuals for students and parents. The parent manual includes a comprehensive section on contraceptives, including medical facts and teenage failure rates. This curriculum is currently used in over 100 different schools in several states as well as in juvenile detention and probation centers. Statistics are available.

Medical organizations

Medical Institute for Sexual Health (MISH)
Joseph S. McIlhaney, Jr., M.D.
P.O. Box 4919
Austin, TX 78765
Phone: (800) 892-9484
This is an information organization that compiles and disseminates data on sexually transmitted diseases.

Resource: "Sexual Health in the 90's" is a ten-minute, hard-hitting video that reveals the facts about "safe sex" and its potentially deadly consequences. It focuses on sexually transmitted diseases and the value of a lifetime, monogamous, and committed relationship.

Americans for a Sound AIDS/HIV Policy
P.O. Box 17433
Washington, DC 20041
This group advocates a responsible approach to stemming the AIDS/HIV epidemic

National Institute for Healthcare Research
6110 Executive Blvd., Suite 908
Rockville, MD 20852
Phone: (301) 984-7162

This organization conducts and publishes research concerning health-care issues.

Other resources

Amie, Inc.
P.O. Box 43631
Birmingham, AL 35243
Phone: 991-9263

Amie Beth Dickinson, Miss Alabama 1994 and now a motivational speaker, travels nationwide addressing groups of teens, parents, educators, and youth leaders about character issues affecting America's young people. She speaks on topics that include:

Reasons to wait and skills to start again
The challenge to build character
Building self-esteem in young ladies
What the future holds (graduation)
Challenge to excellence
Real beauty
The need for character-based education
Choices for single adults

Athletes for Abstinence
A.C. Green Programs for Youth
515 South Figueroa Street, Suite 2000
Los Angeles, CA 90071
Phone: (213) 622-8326

This organization targets junior and senior high school students on campus, at conferences and youth events, and through the media. Programs are presented by teams. Athletes for Abstinence offers "It Ain't Worth It," a 35-minute music documentary on abstinence which features professional athletes who support sexual self-control. The foundation is also working on other presentations on gangs, drugs, and leadership/character issues. Requests for an A.C. Green personal appearance must be made in writing.

Other resources

Bethany Productions
901 Eastern Ave., N.E.
Grand Rapids, MI 49503-1295
Phone: (616) 459-6273

"Second Thoughts" is an award-winning video with dramatic depiction of tensions, concerns, and sexual situations facing middle and high-school youth. A discussion guide and posters are available.

Choices
P.O. Box 2124
Yorba Linda, CA 92686
Phone: (714) 777-3345

This targets junior and senior high school students in public and private schools and focuses on teen sexuality/abstinence. It also provides parents with information on sexual awareness. Presented in a classroom setting for five days, seminars are held locally in the Orange, Los Angeles, and Riverside counties.

Focus on the Family
Educational Resources
P.O. Box 15379
Colorado Springs, CO 80935-3579
Phone: (800) 932-9123

Focus on the Family distributes Sex, Lies . . . and the Truth, a 30-minute video for junior and senior high school students that reveals the hard truth about sex in the nineties. It is available in both public school and Christian versions. Focus on the Family has also prepared an excellent educational study guide for classroom or group instruction as a companion to the video.

Other resources

Free Teens
P.O. Box 97
Westwood, NJ 07675
Phone: (201) 358-1504
"Free Teens" is a presentation on preventing HIV/AIDS and pregnancy. It uses high-impact slides of diseases AIDS patients often develop and examples of AIDS-infected teenagers to convince teens that AIDS is not a problem affecting "other people." It emphasizes the value of parent-child relationships, planning for future life goals, secondary abstinence, peer pressure issues, and role-playing activities.

Gospel Films
Box 455
Muskegon, MI 49443
Phone: (800) 253-0413
"Who Do You Listen To?: Sex In the Age of AIDS" is a film which covers medical facts and how to make good decisions in light of AIDS.

Human Development Research Council, Inc.
3949 Holcomb Bridge Road, Suite 301
Norcross, GA 30092
Phone: (404) 447-1598
"Preview of a Birth" depicts fetal development and is available in video and slides. It includes many photographs by Lennart Milsson, considered the world's leading medical and scientific photographer.

Other resources

Josh McDowell Ministry
P.O. Box 1000 C
Dallas, TX 75221

This organization offers a catalog listing numerous resources on the subjects of sexual abstinence and the need for character in today's young people. McDowell has had the ear of teens, parents, and youth leaders for many years.

Media International
313 East Broadway
Glendale, CA 91209
Phone: (818) 242-5314 or (800) 477-7575

"Power Surge" videos take the fast-paced style of the MTV documentary and apply it to hot topics for teens. It features quick edits, contemporary background music, and interviews. Each video is 15-minutes long. Topics include sex, drugs, friends, dating, depression, AIDS/STDs, parents, and divorce.

New Dimension Films
85895 Loran Highway
Eugene, OR
Phone: (503) 484-7125

"River of Fire" is a video about a couple who made the decision to wait for sex until marriage. It discusses teenage sexuality, pregnancy, and sexually transmitted diseases.

"Control: It's Your Life" targets black teens with a dramatic film presentation that covers attitudes, options, and issues regarding sexuality. It encourages sound decision-making and restraint.

"AIDS: Learn for Your Life" is a film which encourages sexual abstinence to reduce the risk of diseases.

Other resources

Promise University
1230 NE Brockman Place
Seattle, WA 98125
Phone: (800) 669-7972
"You Bet Your Life" multi-media presentation includes a video, overheads, and many other visuals. This one-day workshop is held primarily in churches and private schools.

Sex, Love and Choices
Right to Life League of Southern California
Margaret Birky, Program Director
1028 N. Lake Avenue, Suite 102
Pasadena, CA 91104 (818) 398-6100
Sex, Love, and Choices speaks both to junior and senior high school students on public and private campuses with the abstinence message. The presentations consist of a panel of speakers sharing personal experiences and the importance of abstinence until marriage as a healthy, livable choice.

Summer Nights Communications
John Harris
P.O. Box 28130
Fresno, CA 93729-8130
"AIDS/HIV" is a four-section video series. It stresses abstinence, interviews medical experts, discusses public policy, and provides data.

Other resources

True Love Waits
Southern Baptist Sunday School Board
127 Ninth Avenue, N.
Nashville, TN 37234
Phone: (800) 458-277

This program created a national stir when hundreds of thousands of teens declared through pledges that they would abstain from sex until marriage. True Love Waits has gone international with their message and continues to provide materials for churches and youth groups interested in the program.

Wait on Love
Jeffrey Dean
P.O. Box 120403
Nashville, TN 37212
Phone: (612) 773-7885

This program has a goal to promote and reclaim in youth a positive self-image by encouraging responsible and self-disciplined decisions that overcome negative peer pressure. This program restores a sense of renewed opportunity in youth who have made unwise choices in the past.

Womanity
2141 Youngs Valley Rd.
Walnut Creek, CA 94596
Phone: (415) 943-6424

"Just Wait" is a 14-minute video that helps teens value their virginity. It highlights young men and women sharing their views of sexuality and discusses ways of coping with sexual pressure.

Other resources

Worth the Wait
Youth for Christ
P.O. Box 228822
Denver, CO 80222
Phone: (303) 843-3810, 843-9002 (fax)
This communicates to young people the positive life choice of sexual abstinence until marriage. It promotes this message through rallies and education to youth around America.

Community examples

As I've traveled around the country, I've noticed that some people have come together as a community to bring character education to their young people. Here are some examples I've observed:

Baltimore County Public Schools
Townson, MD 21204
Phone: (410) 887-2063

This large school system integrates values in all curricula areas. Each school's values committee identifies specific values to be stressed for its school population. Materials include How to Establish a Values Education Program in Your School: A Handbook for School Administrators.

In Evansville, Indiana, I participated in a tri-state community effort under the auspices of the Pregnancy Care Network and the Evansville-Vanderburgh School Corporation. Twenty or more institutions put on the "I'm Worth Waiting For" campaign. By speaking in thirty schools, youth clubs, and rallies at churches and universities, I reached over 40,000 young people. My picture was on billboards all over town. Extensive newspaper coverage began one week prior to my arrival. All area radio, TV, and newspaper reporters were invited to a press conference my first day there. The local media produced a series on adoption, and I was on a live talk show for two hours. The community came together to send a message - "I'm worth waiting for."

In Bloomington, Indiana, I was involved in a one-day "Youthfest" which featured bands, music and speeches. The theme was "Pure for Sure," and the governor proclaimed it "Youth Day of Indiana."

Appendix C

Footnotes

Chapter 3

[1] Thomas Lickona, Educating for Character (New York: Bantam Books, 1991), p. 350.
[2] Ann Landers syndicated newspaper column, July 23, 1991. Quoted from Maureen Gallagher Duran, ***Reasonable Reasons to Wait***, Teen Choice Parent/Teacher Manual (An Educated Choice, Inc., 1991), Unit 2, p. 6. Used with permission.
[3] Interview with Dr. Short, July 23, 1991. Ibid, Unit 1, p. 14. Used with permission.
[4] A 1993 study by the American Association of University Women revealed that four out of five high school students—85 percent of girls and 75 percent of boys—said they had been sexually harrassed in schools (Medical Institute of Sexual Health, Austin, TX).
[5] A survey of 1,700 middle schoolers in Rhode Island indicated that 65 percent of boys and 46 percent of girls judged it "acceptable for a man to force sex on a woman" if they have been dating six months or more (MISH).
[6] Joseph A. Califana, Jr., "Teen Pregnancy Can't Be Cured By Medicine Alone" (Birmingham, AL: ***The Birmingham News***, February 13, 1995.
[7] Ibid.

Chapter 4

[1] This story comes from a legal affidavit filed in Jefferson County Circuit Court in Birmingham, Alabama. Names have been changed to protect the privacy of the individuals involved.

[2] Candace C. Crandall, **The Wall Street Journal**, July 31, 1996.

[3] Joan Nelson, **Abortion** (San Diego, CA: Lucent Books, Inc., 1992), p. 27.

[4] "Abortion," Alabama Physicians for Life, brochure.

[5] "An Abortion," **Miami Herald**, Sept. 17, 1989, Topic at page 14. Quoted from Joseph E. Hardison, "Uninformed Consent And Terms Without Definitions," **American Journal of Medicine** 74:932-933, June, 1993. Quoted from "Major Articles and Books Concerning the Detrimental Effects of Abortion" (Charlottesville, VA: The Rutherford Institute, Dec. 1993), p. 41.

[6] Dr. And Mrs. J. C. Willke, **Abortion: Questions & Answers**, (Cincinnati: Hayes Publishing Co., Inc., 1985), p. 44-54.

[7] "Ethics of Testing a Baby's Sex, **USA Today**, Oct. 14, 1987. Quoted from "Major ... Effects Of Abortion" p. 118.

[8] "Abortion," Grolier Electronic Publishing, 1993.

[9] "Abortion," Alabama Physicians for Life, brochure.

[10] Catherine Whitney, **Whose Life**, New York, NY: William Morrow & Co., Inc., 1991), p. 183.

[11] Teri K. Reisser and Paul C. Reisser, M.D., "Identifying and Overcoming Postabortion Syndrome," (Colorado Springs, CO: Focus on the Family, 1992), p. 7, brochure.

[12] Linda Bird Francke, **The Ambivalence Of Abortion** (New York: Random House, 1978). Quoted from "Major Effects Of Abortion, p. 61.

[13] 'Jane Roe' Professes Faith in Christ," **The Alabama Baptist**, August 17, 1995, p. 9.

[14] "Ex-Abortion Provider Reveals Tragic Truth," **Network**, April/May 1995, Vol. 9, No. 2, pp. 1, 8.

[15] "Mother Teresa Visits Capital, **Christianity Today**, April 4,

1994, Vol. 38, Issue 4, p. 75.

[16] "Roe v. Wade Extended," **Insider** (Charlottesville, VA: Rutherford Institute) June 1996.

Chapter 5

[1]. Christa Hones, "The Choice I Made," **Essence**, June 1995, Vol. 26, Issue 2, p. 40.

Chapter 6

[1] "Sex, Lies, And The Truth," Focus On the Family, Colorado Springs, CO., Video.

[2] John Harris, "Fables, Facts, And The Future Of AIDS/HIV," Video.

[3] Thomas Lickona, **Educating for Character** (New York, NY: Bantam Books, 1991), p. 349.

[4] Reasonable **Reasons To Wait**, Unit 4, p. 35.

[5] Joe S. McIlhaney, Jr., "Teens and Sexually Transmitted Diseases," Richard D. Land & Louis A. Moore, editors, **Life at Risk, The Crises in Medical Ethics** (Nashville, TN: Broadman/Holman Publishers, 1995), p. 255-256.

[6] Ibid, p. 256.

[7] American Academy of Pediatrics, Committee on Communications, "Children, Adolescents and Television," Pediatrics, Vol. 87, 1990, p. 1119. (Quoted from **Reasonable Reasons To Wait**, Unit 2, p. 17.)

[8] Marlin Maddoux, **What Worries Parents Most** (Eugene, OR: Harvest House Publishers, 1992), p. 75-76.

[9] From Joe S. McIlhaney, Jr., "Teens and Sexually Transmitted Diseases" Quoted in **Life At Risk, The Crises In Medical Ethics** p. 257-258.

Chapter 7

[1] Jacob Aranza, "A Reason to Wait," Aranza Outreach, LaFayette, LA, brochure.
[2] "If You Think Saying 'No' Is Tough, Just Wait 'Til You say 'Yes,'" U.S. Dept. Of Health and Human Services, Washington, DC, brochure.
[3] Michael J. McManus, "Churches: Wedding Factories or Marriage Savers?" ***National & International Religion Report*** (Vol. 7, No. 23, November 1, 1993), p. 3. Quoted from Jimmy Hester, "News Plus: The Case for Sexual Abstinence Before Marriage," ***The Baptist Standard***, March 2, 1994, p. 8.
[4] Tom Allen, "Will Kids Buy Abstinence?" ***Education Digest***, January 1995, Vol. 60 Issue 5, p. 4-5. Condensed from Virginia Journal of Education, 88 (November 1994), p. 6-12).
[5] ***"Babies who have Babies"*** People, October 24, 1994, p. 55.
[6] Roland, C.M., Rubber Chemistry & Technology, June 1992 Quoted from: Teen Choice brochure, 1994 Project Reality, Falls Church, VA.
[7] R. F. Carey, "Sexually Transmitted Diseases, July/August, 1992. Ibid.
[8] (C. Everett Koop) Surgeon General's "Report on Acquired Immune Deficiency Syndrome," (October 1986). Quoted ***Reasonable Reasons to Wait***, Unit 4, p. 14. Emphasis mine.
[9] Lickona, p. 357.
[10] McManus, p.3.
[11] Lickona, p. 357.
[12] ***Reasonable Reasons To Wait***, Unit 1, p. 25.

Chapter 8

[1] Dr. D. James Kennedy, ***Your Prodigal Child***, (Nashville, TN: Thomas Nelson Publishers, 1988) p. 201.
[2] Bob Gorman, "How can parents help kids make wise choic-

es about sex?" **The Item**, Sumter, SC: Sunday, January 9, 1994, p. 8C.

Chapter 9

[1] (High School Principal), Dolores Curran, **Traits Of A Healthy Family** (San Francisco, CA: Harper & Row, Publishers, 1983), p. 183.
[2] Lickona, back cover of book.
[3] Lickona, p. 85.
[4] Josh McDowell and Bob Hostetler, **Right From Wrong** (Dallas TX: Word Publishing, 1994, p. 80.
[5] Lickona, p. 3.
[6] Joe S. McIlhaney, Jr., "Teens and Sexually Transmitted Diseases," Richard D. Land & Louis A. Moore, editors, **Life at Risk, The Crises in Medical Ethics** (Nashville, TN: Broadman/Holman Publishers, 1995), p. 263.
[7.] Marlin Maddoux, "The Trap of Safe Sex," **What Worries Parents Most** (Eugene, OR: Harvest House Publishers, 1992), p. 84, 86.

Chapter 10

[1] Max Lucado, **A Gentle Thunder** (Dallas, TX: Word Publishing, 1995), p. 52.

Appendix D

Photo Credits

Pages 1-2: Dickinson family collection

Page 3: ***Top left***, Linda Ellen Price; ***Top right***, Charles Sides Photography; ***Bottom left***, Dickinson family collection; ***Bottom right***, Charles Sides photography.

Page 4: ***Top left***, Samford University Photo Department; ***Top right***, Betty Ponder; ***Bottom***, Charles Sides Photography.

Page 5: Charles Sides Photography.

Page 6: Dickinson family collection.

Page 7: ***Top left***, Mobile Registry; ***Top right***, Caroline Bond Estes; ***Center left and right***, Dickinson family collection; ***Bottom left***, Caroline Bond Estes; ***Bottom right***, Dickinson family collection.

Page 8: Karim Shamsi-Basha, Photography.

Cover: David Bartley